Hamlyn All Colour Book of

Puddings
& Desserts

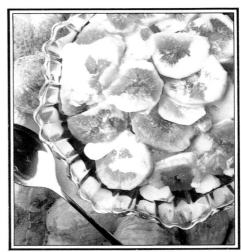

London · New York

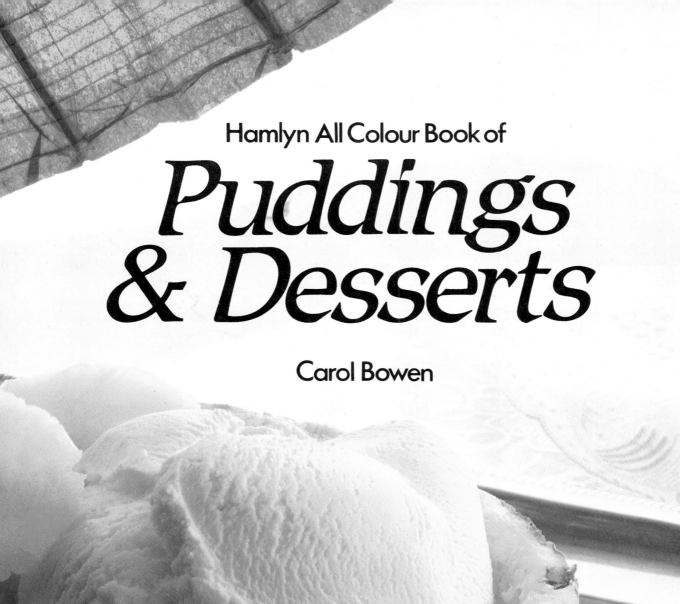

Hamlyn All Colour Book of

Puddings
& Desserts

Carol Bowen

Contents

To my mother and father, Pauline and Arthur.

Photography by Paul Williams
Line illustrations by Marilyn Day

First published in 1982 by
The Hamlyn Publishing Group Limited
London . New York . Sydney . Toronto
Astronaut House, Feltham, Middlesex, England

ISBN 0 600 32271 8

Filmset in Great Britain by Photocomp Ltd,
Birmingham in 10 and 11 pt Apollo 645
Printed in Spain by Graficomo S.A., Córdoba

Useful facts and figures

Notes on metrication

In this book quantities are given in metric and Imperial measures. Exact conversion from Imperial to metric measures does not usually give very convenient working quantities and so the metric measures have been rounded off into units of 25 grams. The table below shows the recommended equivalents.

Ounces	Approx g to nearest whole figure	Recommended conversion to nearest unit of 25
1	28	25
2	57	50
3	85	75
4	113	100
5	142	150
6	170	175
7	198	200
8	227	225
9	255	250
10	283	275
11	312	300
12	340	350
13	368	375
14	396	400
15	425	425
16 (1 lb)	454	450
17	482	475
18	510	500
19	539	550
20 ($1\frac{1}{4}$ lb)	567	575

Note: When converting quantities over 20 oz first add the appropriate figures in the centre column, then adjust to the nearest unit of 25. As a general guide, 1 kg (1000 g) equals 2.2 lb or about 2 lb 3 oz. This method of conversion gives good results in nearly all cases, although in certain pastry and cake recipes a more accurate conversion is necessary to produce a balanced recipe.

Liquid measures The millilitre has been used in this book and the following table gives a few examples.

Imperial	Approx ml to nearest whole figure	Recommended ml
$\frac{1}{4}$ pint	142	150 ml
$\frac{1}{2}$ pint	283	300 ml
$\frac{3}{4}$ pint	425	450 ml
1 pint	567	600 ml
$1\frac{1}{2}$ pints	851	900 ml
$1\frac{3}{4}$ pints	992	1000 ml (1 litre)

Spoon measures All spoon measures given in this book are level unless otherwise stated.

Can sizes At present, cans are marked with the exact (usually to the nearest whole number) metric equivalent of the Imperial weight of the contents, so we have followed this practice when giving can sizes.

Oven temperatures

The table below gives recommended equivalents.

	°C	°F	Gas Mark
Very cool	110	225	$\frac{1}{4}$
	120	250	$\frac{1}{2}$
Cool	140	275	1
	150	300	2
Moderate	160	325	3
	180	350	4
Moderately hot	190	375	5
	200	400	6
Hot	220	425	7
	230	450	8
Very hot	240	475	9

Notes for American and Australian users

In America the 8-oz measuring cup is used. In Australia metric measures are now used in conjunction with the standard 250-ml measuring cup. The Imperial pint, used in Britain and Australia, is 20 fl oz, while the American pint is 16 fl oz. It is important to remember that the Australian tablespoon differs from both the British and American tablespoons; the table below gives a comparison. The British standard tablespoon, which has been used throughout this book, holds 17.7 ml, the American 14.2 ml, and the Australian 20 ml. A teaspoon holds approximately 5 ml in all three countries.

British	American	Australian
1 teaspoon	1 teaspoon	1 teaspoon
1 tablespoon	1 tablespoon	1 tablespoon
2 tablespoons	3 tablespoons	2 tablespoons
3½ tablespoons	4 tablespoons	3 tablespoons
4 tablespoons	5 tablespoons	3½ tablespoons

An Imperial/American guide to solid and liquid measures

Solid measures

IMPERIAL	AMERICAN
1 lb butter or margarine	2 cups
1 lb flour	4 cups
1 lb granulated or castor sugar	2 cups
1 lb icing sugar	3 cups
8 oz rice	1 cup

Liquid measures

IMPERIAL	AMERICAN
¼ pint liquid	⅔ cup liquid
½ pint	1¼ cups
¾ pint	2 cups
1 pint	2½ cups
1½ pints	3¾ cups
2 pints	5 cups (2½ pints)

American terms

The list below gives some American equivalents or substitutes for terms and ingredients used in this book

British/American
Equipment and terms
absorbent kitchen paper/paper towels
baking tray/baking sheet
cling film/saran wrap
cocktail stick/toothpick
cooking foil/aluminium foil
deep cake tin/spring form pan
double saucepan/double boiler
dough/batter
flan tin/pie pan
greaseproof paper/wax paper
grill/broil
patty or bun tins/muffin pans or cups
pudding basin/ovenproof bowl or pudding mould
stoned/pitted
whisk eggs/beat eggs
Ingredients
chocolate, plain/chocolate, semi-sweet
cooking apple/baking apple
crystallised and glacé fruit/candied fruit
desiccated coconut/shredded coconut
digestive biscuits/graham crackers
double cream/heavy cream
gelatine/gelatin
green grapes/white grapes
plain flour/all-purpose flour
raisins, seedless/raisins, seeded
self-raising flour/all-purpose flour sifted with baking powder
shortcrust pastry/basic pie dough
shredded suet/chopped suet
single cream/light cream
soured cream/dairy sour cream
sugar, icing/confectioner's sugar
sultanas/seedless white raisins
yogurt, natural/yogurt, plain

Note: When making any of the recipes in this book, only follow one set of measures as they are not interchangeable.

Introduction

No one would deny that while an appetiser entices the palate for delights to come and has the advantage of being first on the table, and a main course is the anchor on which to base a menu, the pudding or dessert is the meal's crowning glory!

A prestigious position, and one that it regally lives up to. For puddings have no limiting boundaries – there are some for every season, be it midsummer or midwinter; any person, conscientious slimmer or hearty eater; all occasions, from a simple family supper to a scrumptious feast and, chosen carefully, puddings to suit any pocket from the meagre to the extravagant.

Across the world, puddings and desserts have won wide acclaim and every country boasts its own speciality: the French with their delicate crèmes, pastries and gâteaux, the Italians with their creamy ices, the Americans with their unforgettable cheesecakes and, of course, our own steamed and baked puddings and seasonal fruit specialities.

The choices are therefore limitless. But tread carefully into the world of puddings and desserts – for a dish to be highly rated, it must be finely tuned and chosen to complement the dishes that go before it. Choose light fluffy desserts like soufflés, mousses and ice creams when the menu includes a hearty starter or main course, or serve richer desserts in wafer-thin portions. And if a starter or main course is light, then opt for one of the more substantial desserts to satisfy hungry appetites.

Experiment with cook-ahead puddings and desserts: they will leave you free later to concentrate on the other courses, confident and secure that the perfect end to the meal is already 'on ice'. And one must not forget, of course, those carefully timed puddings and desserts that still impress the most travelled gourmets – the flaming crêpes, light-as-air hot soufflés and piping-hot, sugar-crusted fritters.

While writing this book it has become increasingly obvious that we are currently experiencing a pudding and dessert revival and luckily, it would appear, everyone wants to encourage this come-back. Thanks are therefore given to all those friends, too many to mention individually, who shared their family favourites and who unselfishly have allowed me to pass them on to you. Special thanks are also given to Paul Williams for his super photographs which show you just how the final dish will look, whether it be straight from the freezer, refrigerator or oven; Penny Markham for her inventive and creative styling; Pam Cary for her careful editing of what must at times have appeared organised chaos and finally to Jo Tapper for her clever designs and layouts which enable you to find your way easily around the book. Thanks too to Peter, my husband, for not criticising too severely my ever-thickening waistline over the last few months and for his tasting beyond the call of duty.

Carol Bowen

CAROL BOWEN

Harvest lemon cake and Brandy snap creams
(page 112)

Give it a whirl

. . . *with creams, custards, trifles,*
mousses and fools

When all good food affords pleasure, it is desserts that are devised for that purpose alone, and nothing seems to end the meal with more grace and favour than a creamy custard dessert, tempting trifle or mouth-watering mousse or fool. Strikingly different, they can range from the nursery custard to the sophisticated sharp and fruit-flavoured mousse.

Generally soft and smooth in texture, they are best served in glass dishes to show their airy texture and subtle colouring. Or, by contrast, decorate flamboyantly with swirls of whipped cream, chocolate and citrus fruit curls, fruit twists (see pages 121-2) and coarsely chopped nuts.

Layer a trifle carefully to make an impressive striped effect or try moulding some of the more substantial creams and custards like blancmange or crème caramel for a striking appearance that is sure to receive admiring glances. Remember to dampen the inside of the moulds before adding the filling to help turn out the dessert cleanly.

Simple to prepare, especially in advance, creams, custards, mousses and fools can be flavoured quite liberally. Remember, a flavour will diminish considerably in strength once chilled or when cream has been folded through or spread over it. If making well in advance, store or chill carefully and cover to ensure fresh results on the day. Serve these smooth, creamy desserts with crisp sweet biscuits.

Traditional sherry trifle, Orange milk jelly and Pear and honey moscovites (overleaf); Honey fruit fool (page 25)

Traditional sherry trifle

8 trifle sponges
3 tablespoons raspberry jam
25 g/1 oz ratafia biscuits
175 g/6 oz fresh or frozen raspberries, thawed
150 ml/¼ pint sherry
1 tablespoon brandy (optional)
CUSTARD
600 ml/1 pint milk
40 g/1½ oz castor sugar
3 eggs
2 teaspoons cornflour
2-3 drops vanilla essence
300 ml/½ pint double cream
2 teaspoons icing sugar, sifted
fresh raspberries and angelica to decorate

Slice the trifle sponges in half horizontally and spread with the jam. Sandwich back together then place in a deep glass serving dish. Carefully break the ratafia biscuits into small pieces and scatter over the trifle sponges. Top with the raspberries, sprinkle over the sherry and brandy if used and leave to soak for about 30 minutes.

Meanwhile prepare the custard. Place the milk and castor sugar in a saucepan and heat until hot but not boiling. Mix the eggs with the cornflour in a bowl then pour over the hot milk. Stir until well mixed. Return the mixture to the saucepan and cook, over a low heat, until the mixture thickens and coats the back of a wooden spoon. Add the vanilla essence and leave until lukewarm, then pour over the liquor-soaked raspberries. Leave until cold, then chill for 1 hour.

To decorate the trifle, whip the cream with the icing sugar and spread one-third over the top of the trifle. Place the remainder in a piping bag fitted with a star-shaped nozzle and pipe swirls of cream over the top of the trifle. Decorate with fresh raspberries and angelica.

Pear and honey moscovites

2 egg yolks
75 g/3 oz castor sugar
300 ml/½ pint milk
900 g/2 lb cooking pears, peeled, cored and sliced
finely grated rind and juice of 1 lemon
3 tablespoons thick honey
4 teaspoons powdered gelatine
1 egg white
150 ml/¼ pint double cream, whipped

Beat the egg yolks with 25 g/1 oz of the sugar until thick and creamy. Scald the milk in a saucepan and add to the sugar mixture, whisking constantly. Return to the saucepan and cook gently until the custard thickens. Allow to cool.

In another saucepan cook the pears with the lemon rind, lemon juice and honey until reduced to a thick pulp. Purée in an electric blender or pass the pear mixture through a fine nylon sieve, then mix in with the custard.

Place the gelatine in a small bowl with 3 tablespoons water and place the bowl in a saucepan of hot water. Leave until clear and dissolved. Stir into the custard mixture and cool until almost set.

Whisk the egg white until it stands in firm peaks, then fold through the mixture. Pour into six lightly oiled 225-ml/8-fl oz dariole moulds or cups and chill to set.

Prepare the caramel decoration by dissolving the remaining sugar in a saucepan with about 6 tablespoons water. Bring slowly to the boil and cook until the mixture turns a golden caramel. Pour on to an oiled baking tray and allow to set.

To serve, turn out the moscovites and decorate each top with a swirl of whipped cream. Snap the caramel into small pieces and scatter over the cream.

Orange milk jelly

4 teaspoons powdered gelatine
600 ml/1 pint milk
50 g/2 oz castor sugar
2 teaspoons finely grated orange rind
red and yellow food colouring
orange slices to decorate (optional)

Place the gelatine in a small bowl with 3 tablespoons water. Place the bowl in a saucepan of hot water and heat until clear and dissolved.

Scald the milk in a saucepan then add the sugar and orange rind. Heat until the sugar has completely dissolved. Allow to cool slightly, then add the dissolved gelatine, mixing well (see page 120). Tint pale orange with the red and yellow food colouring. Pour into a 900-ml/1½-pint dampened mould and chill until set. Turn out on to a serving plate and decorate with orange slices, if liked, before serving.

Gooseberry crème brûlée

SERVES 4

225 g/8 oz gooseberries, topped and tailed
2-3 tablespoons sugar
600 ml/1 pint natural yogurt
1 teaspoon vanilla essence
pinch of ground nutmeg
4 egg yolks
25 g/1 oz castor sugar
4 tablespoons Demerara sugar

Cook the gooseberries with the sugar and 2 tablespoons water in a saucepan until tender, about 6-8 minutes. Cool and spoon into four individual flameproof dishes.

Mix the yogurt, vanilla, nutmeg, egg yolks and castor sugar together. Place in a bowl over a saucepan of boiling water. Reduce the heat to a simmer and cook, stirring, until the custard coats the back of a spoon. Spoon over the gooseberries and chill until very cold.

Sprinkle the brûlée with the Demerara sugar and stand in a dish filled with ice cubes. (This helps to stop the brûlée bubbling to the surface of the dish during grilling.) Cook under a very hot grill for 1-2 minutes or until the sugar caramelises. Chill until very cold again, before serving. Crack the caramel to serve.

Chocolate blancmange

SERVES 4

3 tablespoons cornflour
600 ml/1 pint milk
75 g/3 oz plain chocolate
40 g/1½ oz castor sugar
1 teaspoon vanilla essence
15 g/½ oz butter

Mix the cornflour to a smooth paste in a bowl with about 6 tablespoons of the milk. Heat the remaining milk with the chocolate in a saucepan until the chocolate has completely dissolved. Pour over the cornflour mixture, whisking constantly. Return to the heat and bring to the boil, stirring all the time. Reduce the heat and simmer for 3 minutes.

Remove from the heat and add the sugar, vanilla and butter and combine well. Pour into a 600-ml/1-pint dampened mould and chill until cold and firm.

To serve, turn out on to a serving dish. Serve with fresh or stewed fruit, if liked.

Speedy raspberry charlotte

SERVES 6-8

450 g/1 lb fresh or frozen raspberries, thawed
1 (135-g/4¾-oz) packet raspberry jelly
300 ml/½ pint boiling water
300 ml/½ pint double cream
1 packet plain langue de chat biscuits
150 ml/¼ pint whipping cream to decorate

Line an 18-cm/7-inch cake tin with greaseproof paper (see page 119). Purée the raspberries in an electric blender, reserving a few for decoration, and sieve to remove any seeds. Dissolve the jelly in the boiling water and leave until cool but not set. Whisk the raspberry purée with the cream until well blended. When the jelly has reached a syrupy consistency, whisk into the raspberry and cream mixture. Turn into the prepared cake tin and chill until set, about 4-6 hours.

To serve, turn the charlotte on to a flat serving dish and remove any greaseproof paper. Carefully press the halved langue de chat biscuits around the edge. Whip the cream until it stands in soft peaks, then pipe or spoon around the top edge of the charlotte. Decorate with the reserved raspberries.

Honey and walnut bavarois

SERVES 6-8

100 g/4 oz ground walnuts
150 g/5 oz butter
4 tablespoons thick honey
450 ml/¾ pint milk
3 egg yolks
100 g/4 oz castor sugar
1 tablespoon powdered gelatine
300 ml/½ pint double cream
3 tablespoons brandy
175 g/6 oz walnut biscuits or digestive biscuits, crushed

Toast the ground walnuts until golden, then allow to cool. Heat 50 g/2 oz of the butter in a saucepan with the honey and milk. Bring to the boil, stirring, add the nuts and leave to stand for 10 minutes.

Beat the egg yolks with 50 g/2 oz of the sugar. Pour over the milk mixture and mix well. Return to the saucepan and cook gently until the mixture coats the back of a spoon. *Do not allow to boil.*

Mix the gelatine in a small bowl with 3 tablespoons water. Place the bowl in a saucepan of hot water and heat until clear and dissolved. Stir into the hot custard mixture and allow to cool. Whip the cream until it stands in soft peaks and fold into the cooled custard with the brandy. Pour into a lightly oiled 1.5-litre/2½-pint fluted ring mould and chill to set.

Melt the remaining butter and mix with the biscuit crumbs and the remaining sugar. Spoon on top of the chilled bavarois, pressing down well. To serve, turn out the bavarois on to a serving plate and serve with fresh fruit.

Creamy plum mould

450 g/1 lb plums, halved and stoned
2 tablespoons finely chopped stem ginger
2 tablespoons sugar
3 teaspoons powdered gelatine
300 ml/½ pint whipping cream
2 egg whites
1 tablespoon sherry

Place the plums in a saucepan with about 2-3 tablespoons water and cook until tender, about 6-8 minutes. Purée the flesh in an electric blender or pass through a fine nylon sieve. Stir in the ginger and sugar.

Place the gelatine in a small bowl with 3 tablespoons water and place the bowl in a saucepan of hot water. Heat until the gelatine is clear and dissolved. Stir into the plum mixture and chill until almost set. Whip the cream until it stands in soft peaks. Whisk the egg whites until they stand in firm peaks. Fold the cream, egg whites and sherry into the plum mixture and turn into a 1.5-litre/2½-pint fancy jelly mould. Chill until set.

To serve, turn out the dessert on to a serving dish. Serve with crisp dessert biscuits and extra stewed or sliced fresh plums, if liked.

Variation

Creamy apricot mould: Prepare as above but use 450 g/1 lb halved and stoned apricots instead of the plums. Serve with crisp dessert biscuits and extra stewed or sliced fresh apricots, if liked.

Cherry-ripe russe

1 (425-g/15-oz) can stoned black cherries
3 tablespoons Kirsch or brandy
16 sponge fingers
2 teaspoons powdered gelatine
300 ml/½ pint double cream
2 tablespoons milk
1 tablespoon castor sugar
fresh cherries to decorate (optional)

Drain the cherries, reserving the juice, and cut each cherry in half. Mix 6 tablespoons of the reserved juice with the Kirsch or brandy. Soak the unsugared side of the sponge fingers in this mixture and use to line the sides of a 1-litre/2-pint fluted mould, sugar side out.

Mix the gelatine with 3 tablespoons of the reserved cherry juice in a small basin and place the basin in a saucepan of hot water. Heat until the gelatine is clear and dissolved.

Meanwhile, whip the cream with the milk, 2 tablespoons cherry juice and sugar until the cream just stands in soft peaks. Fold in the chopped cherries, the gelatine and any remaining Kirsch or brandy mixture. Carefully spoon into the sponge finger-lined mould and chill until set, about 3-4 hours.

To serve, turn the russe out on to a serving dish. Decorate with a few cherries, if available.

Charlotte russe

150 ml/¼ pint made-up lemon jelly
6 candied lemon slices
angelica
24 sponge fingers
300 ml/½ pint milk
4 egg yolks
65 g/2½ oz sugar
pinch of salt
1 teaspoon cornflour
2 teaspoons powdered gelatine
50 ml/2 fl oz lemon juice
grated rind of 1 lemon
300 ml/½ pint double cream

Lightly oil the bottom of a 1-litre/1¾-pint charlotte mould. Pour in a very thin layer of the lemon jelly and chill to set. Place the lemon slices and angelica in a decorative pattern on top of the jelly and pour over the remaining jelly, being careful not to disturb the lemon and angelica from their positions. Chill to set.

Arrange the sponge fingers around the sides of the charlotte mould, sugared side outwards.

Scald the milk. Mix the egg yolks, sugar, salt and cornflour together until light and creamy. Pour the milk over the egg and sugar mixture. Return to the saucepan and cook over a low heat until the custard coats the back of a spoon. *Do not allow to boil.*

Dissolve the gelatine in 2 tablespoons cold water in a bowl placed in a saucepan of hot water and heat until the gelatine is clear and dissolved. Stir into the cooled custard with the lemon juice and lemon rind. Chill the custard until almost set.

Whip the cream until it stands in soft peaks. Fold the cream into the custard and pour into the prepared charlotte mould. Chill until set. Turn out the charlotte on to a dish to serve.

Crème caramel

50 g/2 oz granulated sugar
300 ml/½ pint milk
4 eggs, beaten
25 g/1 oz castor sugar
¼ teaspoon vanilla essence

Lightly grease a 600-ml/1-pint ovenproof dish. Place the sugar in a heavy-based saucepan with 2 tablespoons cold water. Slowly bring to the boil to dissolve the sugar, then boil quickly so that the sugar caramelises and turns a deep golden colour. Immediately add 2 tablespoons boiling water (taking care as the caramel will tend to spit) and pour into the prepared dish. Swirl the caramel around the base of the dish to coat.

Scald the milk in a saucepan and pour over the eggs, whisking continuously. Add the sugar and vanilla. Strain through a fine nylon sieve over the caramel. Bake in a bain-marie or dish with water to come halfway up the sides of the caramel dish, in a moderate oven (160 c, 325 F, Gas Mark 3) for about 50 minutes or until set. Remove from the oven and allow to cool in the dish. Turn out to serve. Crème caramel is best served slightly chilled.

Variation

Individual crème caramels: Prepare as above but pour the caramel and custard mixture into four 150-ml/¼-pint lightly greased metal or ovenproof moulds. Bake as above for 30 minutes.

Apricot chiffon

1 (135-g/4¾-oz) packet lemon jelly
150 ml/¼ pint boiling water
1 (425-g/15-oz) can apricot halves
300 ml/½ pint double cream
16 langue de chat biscuits

Dissolve the jelly in the boiling water. Drain the apricots and add the syrup to the jelly to make it up to 450 ml/¾ pint. Chill until beginning to set.

Reserve 5 apricot halves and chop the rest into quarters. Whip the cream until it stands in soft peaks. Whisk the setting jelly until foamy, then whisk in the cream. Fold in the chopped apricots and turn into a 450-g/1-lb loaf tin. Chill until set.

To serve, turn the apricot chiffon out on to a serving dish. Decorate the sides of the chiffon with langue de chat biscuits and top with the reserved apricots.

21

Strawberry cream syllabub

450 g/1 lb fresh strawberries
6 tablespoons medium dry sherry
300 ml/½ pint double cream
100 g/4 oz castor sugar
grated rind and juice of 1 large lemon

Hull and finely slice all but four of the strawberries. Place in a bowl and sprinkle with 2 tablespoons of the sherry. Leave to macerate for at least 1 hour.

Place the cream, sugar, lemon rind and juice and the remaining sherry in a bowl and whisk until quite thick, about 3 minutes. Place the macerated strawberries in the base of four glasses. Top with the thick syllabub cream and chill for about 30 minutes. Top each with a whole reserved strawberry just before serving.

Variation

Blackberry cream syllabub: Prepare as above but use 450 g/1 lb hulled blackberries instead of the strawberries. Leave whole and macerate in 6 tablespoons blackcurrant liqueur or cordial. Top each syllabub with a reserved blackberry before serving.

Peach syllabub

SERVES 4

5 tablespoons dry white wine
40 g/1½ oz castor sugar
1 tablespoon lemon juice
1 teaspoon finely grated lemon rind
4 ripe peaches, peeled, halved and stoned
150 ml/¼ pint double cream
lemon rind to decorate

Mix the wine, sugar, lemon juice and rind together in a bowl. Thickly slice the peaches and immerse in the wine mixture. Leave to macerate for at least 2 hours.

Drain the peaches with a slotted spoon, reserving the juice. Divide the peaches between four serving glasses. Whip the cream with the reserved juices until it stands in soft peaks. Spoon over the peaches, decorate with lemon rind and serve chilled the same day.

Variation

Nectarine syllabub: Prepare as above but use 4 peeled, halved and stoned nectarines instead of the peaches.

Prune whip

SERVES 4

175 g/6 oz dried prunes, soaked overnight in
600 ml/1 pint cold water
1 egg white
pinch of salt
1½ teaspoons lemon juice
50 g/2 oz castor sugar
grated rind of ½ lemon
50 g/2 oz chopped mixed nuts

Place the prunes with their liquid in a saucepan. Bring to the boil and simmer for 25 minutes until tender. Drain and cool. Stone the prunes and roughly chop the flesh.

Whisk the egg white until it stands in soft peaks. Add the salt and lemon juice and whisk until stiff. Gradually add the castor sugar, whisking continuously, until the mixture stands in firm peaks. Add the prunes and lemon rind and whisk to break up the prunes. Spoon or pipe into four sundae glasses and chill. Serve on the day of making, sprinkled with the chopped mixed nuts.

Variation

Apricot whip: Prepare as above but use 175 g/6 oz dried apricots, soaked overnight in 600 ml/1 pint cold water, instead of the prunes.

Zabaglione

SERVES 4-6

6 egg yolks
6 tablespoons castor sugar
2 teaspoons finely grated orange or lemon rind
6 tablespoons Marsala or sweet white wine

Whisk the egg yolks, sugar and orange or lemon rind together in a bowl until frothy. Stir in the Marsala or white wine and place the bowl over a saucepan of barely simmering water. Whisk until the mixture thickens and rises.

Pour into stemmed glasses and serve at once, decorated with a little extra grated rind, if liked.

Variation

Orange zabaglione: Prepare as above but use 6 tablespoons concentrated orange juice instead of the Marsala or sweet white wine.

Queen Mab's pudding

SERVES 6

600 ml/1 pint milk
finely grated rind of 1 lemon
8 blanched almonds
75 g/3 oz castor sugar
2-3 drops vanilla essence
6 egg yolks
300 ml/½ pint single cream
15 g/½ oz powdered gelatine
50 g/2 oz red, yellow and green glacé cherries,
quartered
40 g/1½ oz citron peel or chopped mixed peel,
finely chopped
15 g/½ oz pistachios or hazelnuts, skins removed
and chopped

Put the milk in a saucepan with the lemon rind, almonds, sugar and vanilla essence and bring almost to the boil. Leave to stand until just hand hot. Meanwhile, beat the egg yolks with the cream in a bowl. Add the hot milk mixture a little at a time and blend well. Return to the top saucepan of a double boiler or place the bowl over a saucepan of hot water. Stir and cook until the custard coats the back of a spoon but *do not allow to boil*. Leave until cool.

Place the gelatine in a small bowl with 3 tablespoons of water. Place the bowl in a saucepan of hot water and leave until the gelatine is clear and dissolved. Stir into the cool custard. Chill the custard until it forms a syrupy texture and is almost set. Quickly stir in the glacé cherries, citrus peel and nuts. Pour into one large or six small glass dishes and serve.

Atholl brose with Danish cones

SERVES 6

ATHOLL BROSE
3 tablespoons whisky
2 tablespoons clear honey
300 ml/½ pint double cream
DANISH CONES
25 g/1 oz butter
1 egg white
30 g/1¼ oz castor sugar
25 g/1 oz plain flour
icing sugar to dust

First prepare the Atholl brose by blending the whisky and honey together in a large mixing bowl. Add the double cream and whisk until light and creamy. Pour into individual glasses and chill until firm.

Meanwhile, prepare the Danish cones. Melt the butter and allow to cool. Whisk the egg white until it stands in firm peaks, add the sugar and whisk again for 3-4 minutes until thick and glossy. Fold the flour into the egg white with the melted butter, incorporating both well. Drop teaspoonfuls of this mixture on to a greased baking tray and spread out to neat oval shapes (only attempt to position and cook four Danish cones on one tray). Dust with a little icing sugar and bake in a moderately hot oven (200 c, 400 f, Gas Mark 6) for 5 minutes until pale golden in the centre but darker around the edges. Immediately lift from the tray with a palette knife and roll into cones. Pop the cones into four small jars – this is a good way of keeping them curled while they harden and form their shape. Cook the remaining cones in the same way and store in an airtight tin until required. Serve with the Atholl brose.

Honey fruit fools

SERVES 4

450 g/1 lb raspberries or strawberries, hulled
2 tablespoons clear honey
300 ml/½ pint double cream
4 tablespoons sweet white wine (optional)

Purée the raspberries or strawberries in an electric blender, reserving a few for decoration. Add the honey and blend again. If you do not have a blender, pass the fruit through a fine sieve, then add the honey.

Whip the cream until it stands in firm peaks and fold into the purée with the wine, if used. Turn into glass dishes and decorate with the reserved fruit. Serve with crisp dessert biscuits.

Variations

Gooseberry or apricot honey fools: Cook 450 g/1 lb gooseberries, topped and tailed, or 450 g/1 lb apricots, peeled and stoned (reserving a few fresh and whole fruits for decoration) in 1-2 tablespoons water for about 10 minutes. Purée and continue as above.

Blackberry or blackcurrant honey fools: Prepare as above but use 450 g/1 lb hulled blackberries or topped and tailed blackcurrants instead of the raspberries or strawberries. Purée, sieve and continue as above.

Strawberry and tangerine mousse

SERVES 6

675 g/1½ lb fresh strawberries, hulled
finely grated rind and juice of 2 tangerines or
small sweet oranges
3 tablespoons icing sugar, sifted
3 egg yolks
100 g/4 oz castor sugar
1 tablespoon powdered gelatine
150 ml/¼ pint whipping cream
2 egg whites

Hull and finely slice 225 g/8 oz of the strawberries and use to line the sides of a 1.5-litre/2½-pint shallow glass dish or six individual glass dishes. Hull and purée 350 g/12 oz of the remaining strawberries in an electric blender and sieve to remove any seeds. Reserve the remaining strawberries for decoration. Mix the purée with the tangerine rind and juice and the icing sugar.

Whisk the egg yolks and sugar until thick and creamy. Whisk in the tangerine and strawberry mixture. Place the gelatine in a small bowl with 3 tablespoons water and place the bowl in a saucepan of hot water. Leave until the gelatine is clear and dissolved. Allow to cool slightly, then fold into the mousse. Whip the cream until it stands in soft peaks and, using a metal spoon, fold into the strawberry mousse.

Whisk the egg whites until they stand in firm peaks, then fold into the mousse. Pour carefully into the dish or glasses so as not to disturb the positioned strawberries. Chill until set, about 2-4 hours.

When set, decorate the mousse with the reserved whole strawberries.

Chocolate and orange mousses

100 g/4 oz plain chocolate
15 g/½ oz butter
4 eggs, separated
2 teaspoons finely grated orange rind
300 ml/½ pint double cream (optional)
grated chocolate and pared orange rind
to decorate

Break the chocolate into small pieces and place in a bowl over a saucepan of boiling water. Stir from time to time so that the chocolate melts. Stir in the butter, allow to melt and mix well. Remove the bowl from the saucepan and add the egg yolks to the chocolate mixture with the orange rind, stirring well to blend.

Whisk the egg whites until stiff and fold through the chocolate mixture. Pour the mousse into individual serving dishes and chill for 2-4 hours until set. It is necessary to chill for several hours to achieve a firm texture.

Serve the mousses with unwhipped double cream and decorate with grated chocolate and pared orange rind. Serve with crisp dessert biscuits.

Loganberry mousses

450 g/1 lb loganberries, topped and tailed
25 g/1 oz powdered gelatine
sugar to taste
300 ml/½ pint double cream

Cook 350 g/12 oz of the loganberries in 3-4 tablespoons water until tender, about 5 minutes. Place the gelatine in a small bowl with 2-3 tablespoons water and leave to soften. Purée the fruit in an electric blender or pass through a sieve, put into a bowl and make up to 600 ml/ 1 pint with water. Adding 1 teaspoon of sugar at a time, sweeten according to taste. Add the gelatine, place over a saucepan of hot water and heat until dissolved. Chill until on the point of setting.

Whip the cream until it stands in soft peaks and fold through the loganberry mixture. Turn into sundae glasses or individual moulds and chill until lightly set. Serve the mousses decorated with the reserved loganberries.

Chocolate rum trifle

1 chocolate Swiss roll
4-5 tablespoons dark rum
1 recipe Chocolate blancmange, cooled
(page 17)
300 ml/½ pint double cream
chocolate flake or chocolate curls to decorate

Slice the Swiss roll thickly and arrange in the base of a trifle dish. Sprinkle over the rum to moisten. Pour over the cooled chocolate blancmange and chill to set.

Whip the cream until it stands in soft peaks then swirl or pipe over the top of the trifle. Decorate with grated chocolate or chocolate curls.

Variation

Caribbean rum trifle: For special occasions top the Swiss roll with 2 thickly sliced bananas, dipped in a little lemon juice. Cover with the blancmange and continue as above.

Coeur à la crème

150 ml/¼ pint double cream
225 g/8 oz full-fat cream cheese
1 egg white
1-2 tablespoons castor sugar
whole strawberries to decorate

Whip the cream until it stands in soft peaks, then beat in the cream cheese to produce a smooth mixture. Whisk the egg white until it stands in firm peaks and fold through the cheese and cream mixture. Stir in the sugar to taste.

Line four heart-shaped moulds or individual perforated moulds with muslin and spoon in the cheese mixture. Leave to drain overnight in the refrigerator.

To serve, turn out the coeurs à la crème, discard the muslin and serve decorated with whole strawberries.

Variation

Belgian coeur à la crème: In Belgium coeur à la crème is generally made with cottage cheese instead of cream cheese. Sieve 225 g/8 oz cottage cheese and mix with 300 ml/½ pint double cream and 50 g/2 oz icing sugar. Fold in 2 stiffly whisked egg whites and pour into the moulds as above. Continue as above.

Mango fool

———— SERVES 4 ————

**2 ripe mangoes
juice of 1 large lime or lemon
150 ml/¼ pint natural yogurt**

Peel the mangoes and cut the flesh away from the stones. Mash or purée in an electric blender until smooth with the lime or lemon juice. Blend in the yogurt and spoon into four individual serving dishes. Chill for about 2 hours before serving with crisp dessert biscuits.

Variation

Banana fool: Prepare as above but use 2 large ripe mashed or puréed bananas instead of the mangoes. Mix with a little lemon juice to prevent the bananas from discolouring. Replace the yogurt with 150 ml/¼ pint lightly whipped double cream for a richer dessert and serve within 2-3 hours of making for best results.

Jamaican jelly creams

———— SERVES 6 ————

**15 g/½ oz powdered gelatine
600 ml/1 pint fresh black coffee
50 g/2 oz soft brown sugar
4 tablespoons Tia Maria
150 ml/¼ pint double cream
1 tablespoon milk
1 tablespoon castor sugar
grated chocolate or chocolate curls to decorate**

Mix the gelatine with the coffee and sugar in a saucepan and heat gently until clear and dissolved. Remove from the heat and add the Tia Maria. Cool, then pour into six serving glasses. Chill to set.

Whip the cream with the milk and castor sugar until it stands in soft peaks. Pipe or swirl over the set coffee jellies and sprinkle with grated chocolate or chocolate curls.

Variation

Caribbean jelly creams: Prepare as above but use crème de cacao instead of the Tia Maria. Sprinkle with crushed chocolate-covered praline.

Tropical ginger and orange trifle

SERVES 6-8

1 (350-g/12-oz) bought Jamaican ginger cake
4 oranges or minneolas, peeled and divided into
segments
8 tablespoons Curaçao or orange juice
4 egg yolks
50 g/2 oz castor sugar
3 tablespoons cornflour
few drops of vanilla essence
600 ml/1 pint milk
3 tablespoons ginger wine or syrup
450 ml/¾ pint double cream
orange slices to decorate (page 122)

Thinly slice the ginger cake and place in the base of a
trifle dish or individual glass bowls. Top with the orange
segments and sprinkle over the Curaçao or orange juice.

In a saucepan combine the egg yolks, castor sugar,
cornflour and vanilla essence. Gradually add the milk and
ginger wine or syrup and bring to the boil. Cook for 2-3
minutes, stirring continuously. Cool and pour over the
trifle base. Chill until lightly set.

Whip the cream until it stands in soft peaks and swirl
or pipe over the top of the trifle. Decorate with orange
slices.

Pawpaw and lime mousse

SERVES 4

1 pawpaw
juice of 1 large lime
150 ml/¼ pint double cream, whipped
sugar to taste
2 teaspoons powdered gelatine
2 egg whites

Cut the pawpaw in half and remove the black seeds.
Using a spoon, scoop out all the flesh and place in a bowl.
Mash or purée the flesh with the lime juice in an electric
blender and blend in the cream and sugar to taste.

Place the gelatine in a small bowl with 2 tablespoons
water and place the bowl in a saucepan of hot water. Heat
until the gelatine dissolves. Cool, then stir into the cream
mixture. Chill until almost set.

Whisk the egg whites until they stand in firm peaks.
Fold into the fruit mixture. Spoon into four individual
dishes and chill to set, about 3 hours. Serve with crisp
dessert biscuits.

Variation

Pawpaw and lemon mousse: When limes are scarce,
simply replace the juice of 1 lime with 3 teaspoons fresh
lemon juice in the recipe above.

Out of the frying pan

. . . come omelettes, crêpes, pancakes and fritters

Omelettes, crêpes and fritters are often considered so elegant and exotic that only a master chef or the most experienced cook should dare to prepare them. Well, crêpes, fritters and omelettes are certainly elegant – maybe even exotic – but some can be so simple to make that even a novice can attempt them.

A crêpe is simply a thin, tender pancake; a fritter a deep or shallow-fried, batter-dipped mixture, and an omelette merely a light and fluffy egg dish. All are easy to prepare at short notice and are the starting point for countless other dishes.

Take the crêpe for example. It can be folded, stacked, rolled and filled with an infinite variety of accompaniments and can be stored in the refrigerator or freezer to await last-minute emergency desserts. An omelette can be just plain sweet, or elegant and rich if filled with fruit and cream. Not forgetting, of course, the plain pancake, though not so plain if you roll it in sugar and spice and all things nice!

A good crêpe or omelette pan will prove a worthwhile investment and a good thick-based, sturdy, deep frying pan is a must, but beyond that all you need is imagination. The following recipes should prove a tasty starting point.

Crêpes Suzette and Sweet soufflé omelette (overleaf)

Crêpes Suzette

SERVES 4-6

PANCAKE BATTER
100 g/4 oz plain flour
pinch of salt
grated rind of ½ lemon
1 egg
300 ml/½ pint milk or milk and water
15 g/½ oz butter, melted
butter for frying
ORANGE BUTTER SAUCE
5-6 sugar cubes
2 large oranges
75 g/3 oz butter
50 g/2 oz castor sugar
1 tablespoon orange juice
1 tablespoon Cointreau
2-3 tablespoons brandy

If you have a chafing dish, let your guests or family enjoy watching you finish this delicious French flambé dish of pancakes in orange butter sauce. If you don't have a pan pretty enough for public scrutiny (or if you're not sufficiently extrovert to want to display your skills), simply heat the pancakes and sauce in the oven and pour the flaming brandy over when you take it to the table. Either way, you can do the main preparation the day before, if you wish.

First prepare the pancakes by sifting the flour and salt together in a bowl. Add the lemon rind, make a well in the centre of the mixture and break in the egg. Gradually add half the liquid, beating well until the batter is smooth. Add the remaining liquid and the melted butter and beat until well mixed.

Heat a little butter in an 18-cm/7-inch heavy-based frying pan or omelette pan. When it is really hot, tilt the pan so that the butter runs round and completely coats the sides of the pan; pour off any surplus. Pour in just enough batter to cover the base of the pan thinly and cook quickly until golden brown underneath. Turn with a spatula or by tossing and cook the second side until golden. The pancakes for this dish should be really thin and lacy. As the pancakes are cooked, stack flat on a plate with a sheet of greaseproof paper between each one to prevent sticking. Cover and keep warm.

To make the sauce, remove the zest from the oranges by rubbing the sugar cubes over the rind until they are soaked in orange 'oil'. Cut a few thin strips of orange zest to add to the sauce later for decoration. Crush the sugar cubes and add them to the butter with the castor sugar. Beat until soft and creamy and then add the orange juice and Cointreau. Work again until thoroughly mixed. Chill until required.

To serve the crêpes in a chafing dish, melt the orange butter over a gentle heat. When melted, pour half the butter into the chafing dish and light the flame underneath. Take one pancake at a time and place it in the dish, spoon over the sauce, fold the pancake in half then half again and push to the side of the pan. Repeat with more pancakes until the pan is full. This will have to be done in two batches. Pour brandy into a tablespoon, gently heat the bowl of the spoon with a lighted match to warm the brandy, pour it over the pancakes in the

chafing dish and ignite. Serve at once. Repeat with the remaining butter and pancakes.

To prepare without using a chafing dish, place a little of the chilled orange butter in the middle of each pancake, fold into four and arrange them in a shallow ovenproof serving dish. Melt the remaining orange butter and pour over the pancakes. Cover with cooking foil then bake in a cool oven (150 C, 300 F, Gas Mark 2) for 30 minutes.

To serve, remove the cooking foil, warm the brandy gently as above, pour over the pancakes and ignite. Serve at once.

Sweet soufflé omelette

SERVES 1

2 eggs, separated
1 teaspoon castor sugar
butter for frying
3 tablespoons fruit purée (optional)
1 tablespoon icing sugar, sifted

Whisk the egg yolks until creamy with 2 tablespoons water. Whisk the egg whites until stiff with the sugar. Fold the egg yolk mixture through the egg white, taking care not to lose too much air. Melt a little butter in the base of a 20-cm/8-inch frying pan or omelette pan and swirl around the base to coat. Pour in the egg mixture and cook over a moderate heat until the underside is golden. Place under a hot grill and cook until slightly risen and just set. Run a knife around the edge of the omelette and under the base. Spread with the fruit purée, if used, and double the omelette over. Slide on to a warmed serving plate and dust with the icing sugar. Serve at once.

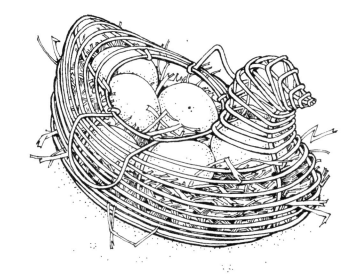

Lemon beignets

SERVES 4-6

LEMON SAUCE
75 g/3 oz sugar
1 teaspoon cornflour
25 g/1 oz butter
grated rind and juice of 1 lemon
BEIGNETS
1 recipe Choux pastry (page 81)
oil for deep frying
castor sugar to sprinkle

First prepare the sauce by mixing the sugar and cornflour together. Gradually mix in 300 ml/$\frac{1}{2}$ pint water and place in a saucepan. Bring to the boil, stirring, remove from the heat and add the butter, lemon rind and juice.

Prepare the choux pastry according to the recipe instructions and heat the oil to 190 C/375 F. Fry teaspoons of the pastry in the oil until cooked through and golden brown, about 3-5 minutes. The beignets will look very attractive if the pastry is piped through a fluted nozzle, cut off in small pieces and fried. Drain on absorbent kitchen paper and sprinkle with castor sugar. Serve the hot beignets with the warm lemon sauce.

Hot fudge sundae crêpes

SERVES 4

1 recipe Pancake batter (opposite page)
1 recipe Rich vanilla ice cream (page 98) or
600 ml/1 pint bought vanilla ice cream
1 recipe Fudge sauce (page 99)
150 ml/$\frac{1}{4}$ pint double cream, whipped
2 tablespoons chopped mixed nuts
maraschino cherries to decorate

Prepare the pancakes according to the recipe instructions. For each sundae, place 2-3 small scoops of ice cream in the centre of each crêpe. Fold up the sides to make a roll. Place in a serving dish. Pour over the hot fudge sauce. Top with whipped cream and sprinkle with a few nuts. Decorate with maraschino cherries and serve at once.

Crêpes Georgette

SERVES 6

1 recipe Pancake batter (page 32)
1 recipe Confectioner's custard (page 106)
6 slices fresh pineapple, chopped
25 g/1 oz butter, melted
icing sugar to dust
4 tablespoons brandy

Prepare the pancakes according to the recipe instructions and keep them warm. Mix the cold Confectioner's custard with the pineapple and use to fill the crêpes. Place side by side in an ovenroof dish and brush with the melted butter. Dust with the icing sugar. Heat a metal skewer until very hot and use it to mark a criss-cross pattern on top of the crêpes (see page 121) or, if preferred, cook under a hot grill for about 5 minutes to caramelise the sugar.

Heat the brandy in a small pan, ignite and pour over the crêpes. Serve at once.

Variation

Sizzling peach crêpes: Prepare as above but use 6 peeled and sliced peaches instead of the pineapple.

Caramel banana crêpes flambé

SERVES 4

1 recipe Pancake batter (page 32)
50 g/2 oz butter
25 g/1 oz brown sugar
6 ripe bananas, peeled and thickly sliced
5 tablespoons dark rum
whipped cream to serve

Prepare the pancakes according to the recipe instructions and keep them warm. Melt the butter in a frying pan with the sugar. Stir in the bananas and cook until the bananas soften slightly, about 2-3 minutes. Fill the crêpes with the banana mixture.

Place the rum in a small pan, ignite and pour over the crêpes. Serve at once with whipped cream.

Variation

Caramel pear crêpes flambé: Prepare as above but use 4 peeled, cored and sliced pears instead of the bananas. Cook until the pears soften slightly, about 5-6 minutes.

Poor knights of Windsor

8 slices white bread, crusts removed
50 g/2 oz butter
6 tablespoons strawberry jam
3 tablespoons sweet white wine
1 egg, beaten
150 ml/¼ pint milk
50 g/2 oz butter
1 tablespoon oil
1 tablespoon castor sugar

Spread the bread slices with the butter and sandwich together with the jam. Cut into thick fingers and dip quickly in the wine. Beat the egg and milk together in a bowl and dip the fingers into this mixture using a slotted spoon.

Heat the butter and oil in a frying pan, adding a little more butter during cooking if necessary. Fry until the fingers are golden on both sides. Drain on absorbent kitchen paper and dust with the castor sugar. Serve warm.

Dorset cream toasts

1 egg yolk
150 ml/¼ pint single cream
2 teaspoons castor sugar
grated rind of ½ lemon
6 slices French bread, cut into
2.5-cm/1-inch thick slices
2 eggs
25 g/1 oz butter
2 tablespoons oil
castor sugar to dust
orange or lemon quarters to serve (optional)

Place the egg yolk in a shallow dish and mix with the single cream, castor sugar and lemon rind. Place the bread in the dish and leave to soak for about 5 minutes.

Beat the eggs and dip the soaked bread slices in the egg. Heat the butter and oil in a frying pan until sizzling. Add the bread slices and cook until golden on the underside. Using a spatula flip over and cook for a further 1-2 minutes. Remove from the pan, drain on absorbent kitchen paper and dust with a little castor sugar. If liked, serve with orange or lemon quarters to squeeze.

Apple fritters

SERVES 4

4 large apples, peeled, cored and cut into
½-cm/¼-inch thick rings
100 g/4 oz vanilla sugar
FRITTER BATTER
100 g/4 oz plain flour
¼ teaspoon salt
1 tablespoon oil
1 egg, separated
150 ml/¼ pint milk or milk and water
oil for deep frying
icing sugar to sprinkle

Dip the apple rings in vanilla sugar and leave to dry slightly on absorbent kitchen paper.

Prepare the fritter batter by sifting the flour and salt together into a bowl. Make a well in the centre and pour in the oil and egg yolk. Gradually draw the flour into the egg, adding the milk a little at a time, beating to produce a smooth batter. Whisk the egg white until it stands in firm peaks and fold into the batter mixture.

Heat the oil to 190 C/375 F and coat the apple rings in the batter. Fry the apple rings in the oil for about 4 minutes or until golden and cooked through. Drain on absorbent kitchen paper. Sprinkle with icing sugar and serve.

Note: Make your own vanilla sugar by storing a vanilla pod in a jar of castor sugar. The sugar will be permeated by a delicate vanilla flavour, and you can use it for making puddings and desserts.

Rum and honey pear fritters

SERVES 4-6

BATTER
100 g/4 oz plain flour
1 tablespoon oil
2 egg whites
FRITTERS
4 tablespoons clear honey
1½ tablespoons dark rum
juice and finely grated rind of 1 orange
450 g/1 lb firm dessert pears, peeled, cored and
cut into thick rings
oil for deep frying
150 m/¼ pint double cream

First prepare the batter by mixing the flour with 150 ml/¼ pint tepid water and the oil. Leave to stand for about 1 hour.

Meanwhile, mix the honey, rum and orange juice and rind together in a large bowl. Add the pears and leave to macerate for at least 30 minutes. Drain, using a slotted spoon and reserving the juices. Dust the pear rings with a little flour.

Heat the oil to 190 C/375 F. Whisk the egg whites until stiff and fold into the batter. Coat the pear rings with the batter mixture and fry in the hot oil until golden, about 3-5 minutes. Drain on absorbent kitchen paper.

Whip the cream until it stands in soft peaks and fold in the reserved juices. Serve the fritters accompanied by the cream.

Rum babas

SERVES 16

25 g/1 oz fresh yeast
6 tablespoons warm milk
225 g/8 oz strong white flour
½ teaspoon salt
25 g/1 oz castor sugar
4 eggs, beaten
100 g/4 oz butter, softened
4 tablespoons clear honey
2 tablespoons dark rum
300 ml/½ pint double cream
glacé cherries to decorate

Lightly grease 16 small ring moulds. Cream the yeast with milk and mix in 50 g/2 oz of the flour. Leave in a warm place until frothy, about 20 minutes.

Place the yeast mixture in a bowl and beat in the remaining flour, salt, sugar, eggs and butter. Beat for about 3-4 minutes.

Half fill the moulds with the batter, cover with cling film and leave in a warm place until the batter rises to fill two-thirds of the moulds.

Bake in a moderately hot oven (200 c, 400 f, Gas Mark 6) for 12-15 minutes. Turn out and cool on a wire rack.

Prepare the baba syrup by heating the honey with 4 tablespoons water and the rum. Stir over a low heat until well mixed. Spoon the syrup over the still hot babas. Leave to cool.

To serve, whip the cream until it stands in soft peaks and pipe or spoon the cream into the centres of the babas. Decorate with glacé cherries before serving.

Fried apple and sultana parcels

SERVES 4

PANCAKES
100 g/4 oz plain flour
pinch of salt
2 eggs
300 ml/½ pint milk
oil for frying
FILLING
2 (125-g/4-oz) cans apple purée
3 teaspoons ground cinnamon
50 g/2 oz sultanas
25 g/1 oz butter
2 tablespoons oil
25 g/1 oz castor sugar

Sift the flour and salt into a bowl and gradually add the eggs and milk to make a smooth batter. Melt a little oil in an 18-cm/7-inch frying pan and pour in a little of the batter, tilting quickly to thinly cover the base of the pan. Cook until the underside is golden then turn over with a spatula. Cook for a further 20 seconds. Remove and stack on greaseproof paper. Continue to cook the remaining batter in the same way.

To make the filling, mix the apple purée and 1 teaspoon of the cinnamon together with the sultanas. Spread over each pancake and fold into a parcel. Melt the butter in a frying pan with the oil and fry the pancake parcels until brown on both sides. Drain on absorbent kitchen paper and dust with the remaining cinnamon mixed with the castor sugar. Serve at once.

Stacked peach and ginger pancakes

SERVES 6

PANCAKES
100 g/4 oz plain flour
pinch of salt
1 egg, beaten
300 ml/½ pint milk
1 tablespoon oil
oil to fry
FILLING
25 g/1 oz butter
675 g/1½ lb peaches, peeled, stoned and sliced
50 g/2 oz brown sugar
½ teaspoon ground ginger
50 g/2 oz raisins
GLAZE
4 tablespoons apricot jam, warmed
25 g/1 oz hazelnuts, chopped

Sift the flour and salt into a bowl. Make a well in the centre and add the egg. Gradually draw the flour into the egg, adding a little milk. Beat until smooth, adding the rest of the milk and the tablespoon of oil. Leave to stand for 30 minutes.

Heat a 15-cm/6-inch frying pan or omelette pan and add a few drops of oil. Pour in a little of the batter, tilting the pan quickly to cover the base thinly. Cook until the bottom of the pancake is golden. Using a spatula, turn over and continue to cook for about 20 seconds. Remove from the pan, place on greaseproof paper and continue to make the pancakes with the remaining batter.

To prepare the filling, melt the butter in a saucepan. Add the peaches, sugar, ginger, raisins and about 2 tablespoons water. Cook for about 10 minutes or until the peaches are tender.

Place one pancake on a greased ovenproof dish. Cover with a little of the peach mixture and another pancake. Continue to stack the pancakes with the filling until both are used up. Spoon over the warmed apricot jam and bake in a moderate oven (180 C, 350 F, Gas Mark 4) for 12-15 minutes. Sprinkle with the hazelnuts and serve cut into wedges. Serve with whipped cream or natural yogurt.

Sweet and sour fruit pancakes

SERVES 6

PANCAKES
100 g/4 oz plain flour
2 teaspoons icing sugar, sifted
pinch of salt
1 egg, beaten
450 ml/¾ pint milk
oil or butter for frying
SAUCE
50 g/2 oz butter
200 g/7 oz icing sugar, sifted
5 tablespoons concentrated frozen orange
juice, thawed
2 tablespoons grated orange rind
300 ml/½ pint soured cream
fresh orange segments to decorate

Prepare the pancake batter by mixing the flour with the sugar and salt. Make a well in the centre of the mixture and add the egg. Gradually draw in the flour, adding the milk to make a smooth batter. Heat a little oil in an 18-cm/7-inch frying pan and add a little of the batter. Tilt the pan quickly to coat the base thinly with batter. Cook the pancake until golden on the underside. Turn it over with a spatula and cook the pancake for a further 20 seconds. Remove and place on greaseproof paper. Continue to make the pancakes with the remaining batter. Keep warm.

To make the sauce, melt the butter in a saucepan. Add the icing sugar, orange juice and orange rind, blending them well to make a smooth sauce. Heat to boiling point.

To serve, spread the pancakes with a little of the soured cream. Roll up and place on a heated serving dish. Pour over the sauce and decorate with fresh orange segments.

Spiced apricot pancakes

SERVES 6

300 ml/½ pint medium dry white wine
175 g/6 oz dried apricots
175 g/6 oz fresh white breadcrumbs
¼ teaspoon ground cloves
¼ teaspoon ground mixed spice
½ teaspoon ground mace
pinch of salt
60 g/2½ oz castor sugar
300 ml/½ pint double cream
5 eggs, beaten
2 teaspoons rosewater
75 g/3 oz butter
2 oranges, peeled and divided into segments
25 g/1 oz icing sugar, sifted

Heat the wine until almost boiling then pour over the apricots. Leave to stand for 30 minutes.

Meanwhile, mix the breadcrumbs, spices, salt and sugar in a bowl and make a well in the centre. Mix the cream and eggs together and pour into the well. Gradually work into the breadcrumb mixture, beating well to blend. Leave to stand for 30 minutes.

Remove the apricots from the wine with a slotted spoon, reserving the wine. Stir the apricots into the batter with the rosewater. Melt the butter in a 28-cm/11-inch frying pan or omelette pan. Pour in all the batter and cook over a medium heat until golden on the underside. Place under a hot grill and cook the top until it turns golden brown and has set. Slide on to a warmed serving plate. Dust with a little icing usgar and scatter over the orange segments. Cut into wedges to serve with the reserved warm wine.

American blueberry pancakes

SERVES 4

1 egg
300 ml/½ pint milk
1 tablespoon castor sugar
pinch of salt
125 g/4½ oz plain flour
grated rind of ½ lemon
225 g/8 oz canned blueberries, drained
oil for frying
warm honey to serve

Beat the egg with the milk, sugar and salt. Place the flour in a bowl, make a well in the centre and add a little of the egg mixture. Gradually draw the flour into the egg, beating in the remaining egg mixture to make a smooth batter. Leave to stand for 30 minutes, then fold in the lemon rind and some of the blueberries.

Heat a little oil in the base of an 18-cm/7-inch frying pan. Pour in a small ladleful of batter to cover the base of the pan and cook until the pancake is golden brown on the underside. Using a spatula, turn over and cook for a further 1 minute. Keep it warm while cooking the remaining pancakes in the same manner. Warm the remaining blueberries in a small pan, fill the pancakes and serve with warm honey.

Pancakes with raspberry cream

SERVES 4

1 recipe Pancake batter (page 32)
350 g/12 oz raspberries, hulled
150 ml/¼ pint double cream
225 g/8 oz cream cheese
sugar to taste
2 tablespoons Kirsch (optional)

Prepare the pancakes according to the recipe instructions and keep them warm.

Purée almost all the raspberries in an electric blender, reserving a few for decoration, then pass through a fine nylon sieve. Whip the purée with the cream and cream cheese until thick. Sweeten to taste and add the Kirsch, if liked.

Fill the pancakes with the raspberry cream and serve at once. Decorate with the reserved fresh raspberries.

Variation

Pancakes with strawberry cream: Prepare as above but use 350 g/12 oz hulled strawberries instead of the raspberries.

Scotch pancakes with lemon sauce

SERVES 4-6

PANCAKES
100 g/4 oz self-raising flour
25 g/1 oz castor sugar
1 egg, beaten
2 tablespoons lemon juice
5 tablespoons milk
a little melted butter

LEMON SAUCE
100 ml/4 fl oz lemon juice
1 tablespoon arrowroot
50-75 g/2-3 oz castor sugar
25 g/1 oz butter

To make the pancakes, sift the flour into a bowl and stir in the sugar. Make a well in the centre of the mixture and add the egg. Add the lemon juice and 2 tablespoons of the milk. Beat until well mixed, then gradually add the remaining milk to make a smooth batter. Heat a griddle or heavy-based frying pan over moderate heat, and brush lightly with a little melted butter. Drop tablespoons of the batter on to the heated griddle or frying pan and cook for about 2 minutes, or until bubbles appear and a 'skin' forms on the surface of the pancakes. Turn over carefully with a spatula and continue to cook for 1-2 minutes, or until the remaining side is golden. Keep warm.

Meanwhile prepare the lemon sauce. Place the lemon juice in a measuring jug and make up to 300 ml/½ pint with water. In a small saucepan mix the arrowroot to a smooth paste with a little of the lemon juice mixture. Add the sugar (according to taste), butter and remaining lemon juice. Bring to the boil, stirring constantly. Simmer for 2-3 minutes then serve with the pancakes.

Pick of the crop

. . . super ways with fruit puddings, salads and jellies

At the beginning of time, in the Garden of Eden, Eve tempted Adam with an apple . . . it is hardly surprising that we now tempt our families and guests alike with fruit-based or fruit-filled puddings and desserts.

Fruit is a constant source of delight for most cooks, since it offers such variety. Perhaps the secret of success is to follow the seasons, for each new month introduces a new type of fruit. Raspberries, strawberries and other berry fruits, while generally available all year round, reach their finest flavour in high summer, yet rhubarb is at its best in late winter or early spring. Experiment, too, with imported specialities such as kiwi fruit, mangoes and pawpaws. You will find them just as delicious as your own home-grown apples, pears and plums and they will soon become family favourites just as the orange, pineapple and tangerine have done before them.

Choose fruit carefully for puddings and desserts – it must be just as fresh as fruit chosen for plain eating. Avoid any with bruised skin and an old appearance and you cannot go far wrong. You can also use it to decorate other desserts. A simple lemon twist, for instance, on an ordinary cheesecake will literally transform it from the plain to the luxury class.

Using fruit in season for tasty desserts makes good economical sense as well as being sound nutritionally and nature will also ensure that it has the virtue of variety.

Clockwise from the top: *Fresh fruit salad, Caramelised oranges, Dried fruit salad and Claret jelly (overleaf)*

Fresh fruit salad

SUGAR SYRUP
100 g/4 oz sugar
150 ml/¼ pint water
juice of ½ lemon
FRUIT SALAD
2 dessert apples, cored and sliced
3 oranges, peeled, pith removed and segmented
50 g/2 oz black grapes, seeds removed
50 g/2 oz green seedless grapes
225 g/8 oz raspberries or strawberries, hulled
2 kiwi fruits, peeled and sliced (optional)
2 plums, stoned and sliced
2 bananas, peeled and sliced

Prepare the syrup by placing the sugar, water and lemon juice in a small saucepan. Bring gently to the boil and simmer for 3 minutes. Allow to cool.

Mix the prepared fruits together in a large serving bowl and pour over the syrup. Chill for 1 hour before serving.

Caramelised oranges

SERVES 4

175 g/6 oz granulated sugar
8 seedless oranges

First prepare a caramel by heating the sugar with 75 ml/ 3 fl oz water in a small saucepan. Bring to the boil and cook steadily until a rich brown caramel is produced. Immediately, carefully add 100 ml/4 fl oz water and stir gently, over a low heat, until the caramel has melted. Leave to cool. If the caramel syrup is too thick, add a little more water to give a coating consistency.

Pare the rind from one of the oranges and cut the rind into thin julienne strips. Blanch in boiling water for 2 minutes, drain and cool. Cut the peel and white pith from all the oranges then carefully slice each orange evenly across the diameter. Re-form the oranges back to their original shape and secure with wooden cocktail sticks. Place in a serving dish and scatter over the orange rind. Pour over the caramel syrup and chill for 1 hour. Caramelised oranges are delicious served with brandy snaps filled with whipped cream.

Dried fruit salad

SERVES 4

350 g/12 oz dried fruits (for example apples, prunes, bananas, pears, figs, apricots and raisins), soaked overnight in cold water
3 tablespoons golden syrup
300 ml/½ pint medium dry sherry or cider
juice of 1 orange
double cream or natural yogurt to serve

Drain the fruit and place in an ovenproof dish. Mix the golden syrup, sherry or cider together with the orange juice. Pour over the fruit, cover and cook in a moderate oven (180 C, 350 F, Gas Mark 4) for 45 minutes. Remove and serve hot or cold with the cream or natural yogurt poured over the top.

Claret jelly

SERVES 6

15 g/½ oz powdered gelatine
300 ml/½ pint hot water
100 g/4 oz castor sugar
225 g/8 oz redcurrant jelly
300 ml/½ pint claret
2 tablespoons lemon juice

Sprinkle the gelatine over the water in a saucepan and heat gently until the gelatine has dissolved. Gradually add the sugar and redcurrant jelly, stirring constantly until dissolved. *Do not allow to boil.* Strain through muslin or a fine nylon sieve into a bowl and cool. Add the claret and lemon juice. Pour the jelly into a dampened 900-ml/1½-pint jelly mould and chill until set.

To serve, dip the jelly mould in hot water for a few seconds and invert on to a serving dish. Serve with cream and sponge fingers.

Variations

Orange jelly: Follow the recipe above but substitute orange marmalade for the redcurrant jelly and orange juice for the claret. If you wish to set orange slices in the jelly, layer by layer, increase the gelatine content to 25 g/ 1 oz.

Port wine jelly: Follow the recipe above but substitute port wine for the claret.

Redcurrant cups

SERVES 6

2 teaspoons powdered gelatine
9 tablespoons redcurrant jelly
225 g/8 oz redcurrants, topped and tailed
150 ml/¼ pint double cream
3 tablespoons milk
2 teaspoons arrowroot
fresh redcurrants to decorate

Place the gelatine in a small bowl with 4½ tablespoons water. Place the bowl in a saucepan of hot water and leave until the gelatine is clear and dissolved. Meanwhile, in a saucepan heat 3 tablespoons of the redcurrant jelly with the redcurrants until they are soft. Purée in an electric blender then pass through a fine nylon sieve. Stir the dissolved gelatine into the redcurrant purée.

Whip the cream with the milk until it stands in soft peaks. Using a metal spoon, fold the cream into the purée. Pour into six small glass cups and chill to set.

When set, heat the arrowroot in a saucepan with 6 tablespoons water and the remaining redcurrant jelly. Bring to the boil, stirring constantly until the mixture thickens and clears. Cool slightly, then pour over the individual redcurrant creams, decorate with fresh redcurrants and chill until set.

Summer fruit compote

SERVES 4-6

175 g/6 oz castor sugar
600 ml/1 pint water
900 g/2 lb prepared soft summer fruits
(for example, raspberries, strawberries,
redcurrants, blackcurrants, loganberries,
gooseberries, blackberries and cherries)
1 tablespoon cornflour

Place the sugar and water in a saucepan and heat until the sugar has dissolved. Bring to the boil. Carefully add the fruits which need the longest cooking time (the goose-berries, for example), then gradually add the softer summer fruits that need the minimum amount of cooking. Cook for a maximum of 3-4 minutes, then with a slotted spoon transfer them to a serving dish and reserve the syrup.

Blend the cornflour with a little cold water and stir into the syrup. Bring to the boil, stirring constantly, until a slightly thickened syrup is formed. Remove from the heat, pour over the fruit and allow to cool. Chill before serving with whipped cream.

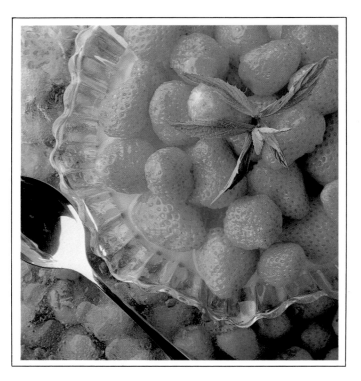

Strawberries Romanoff

SERVES 4

675 g/1½ lb strawberries, hulled
100 g/4 oz castor or icing sugar, sifted
100 ml/4 fl oz orange juice
50 ml/2 fl oz Curaçao (optional)

Place the strawberries in a bowl and sprinkle with the castor or icing sugar. Pour over the orange juice and Curaçao if used. Turn the fruit over in the juices then chill for at least 1 hour. Decorate with fresh mint leaves, if liked.

Variation

Raspberries or mulberries Romanoff: Prepare as above but use 675 g/1½ lb hulled raspberries or mulberries instead of the strawberries.

Drunken grapes

SERVES 6

225 g/8 oz green grapes
3-4 tablespoons brandy
300 ml/½ pint double cream
8 tablespoons Demerara sugar

Peel, halve and remove the pips from the grapes. Place in a bowl and macerate in the brandy for 2-4 hours.

Lightly whip the cream. Transfer the grapes to six small ovenproof dishes and cover with the cream. Sprinkle over the Demerara sugar and cook under a very hot grill until the sugar caramelises. Chill for at least 2 hours before serving.

Variation

Drunken plums: Prepare as above but use 225 g/8 oz peeled, halved and stoned sweet plums instead of the grapes. Chop into bite-sized pieces before macerating in the brandy.

Apricots in Armagnac

SERVES 12

675 g/1½ lb dried apricots
1 (600-ml/1-pint) bottle Armagnac

Place the apricots in an ovenproof dish and heat through in a cool oven (150 C, 300 F, Gas Mark 2) for 15 minutes.

While still hot, place the apricots in a 1-litre/1¾-pint preserving jar and fill two-thirds full with the Armagnac. Seal and store for 1 week.

Re-open after a week and pour in the remaining Armagnac. Seal and store for at least 2 months. Serve with vanilla ice cream and crisp dessert biscuits, if liked. Apricots in Armagnac also make a delightful gift when stored in decorative preserving jars.

Variations

Prunes in Armagnac: Dried prunes may be substituted for the apricots. Pierce each prune with the tip of a knife right through to the stone. Heat through in a cool oven and continue as above.
Peaches, apricots and prunes in Armagnac: Prepare as above but use a mixture of 225 g/8 oz dried peaches, 225 g/8 oz dried apricots and 225 g/8 oz dried prunes instead of apricots.

Fresh figs in port and cream

SERVES 4

450 g/1 lb fresh green or pink figs,
peeled and sliced
150 ml/¼ pint port
1 tablespoon brandy (optional)
1 tablespoon Curaçao (optional)
150 ml/¼ pint double cream

Place the figs in a shallow serving dish. Cover with cling film and chill for 30 minutes. Add the port and the brandy and Curaçao if used. Carefully pour over the cream. Mix gently just before serving.

Variation

Guavas in port and cream: Prepare as above but use 1 large can peeled guavas instead of the figs. Drain the guavas from their syrup and slice thickly before adding the port and cream.

Summer pudding

SERVES 4-6

450 g/1 lb raspberries, hulled
225 g/8 oz redcurrants, topped and tailed
225 g/8 oz blackcurrants, topped and tailed
100 g/4 oz blackberries, hulled
225 g/8 oz castor sugar
6 tablespoons boiling water
14 thin slices bread, crusts removed

Summer pudding is a chilled, scarlet-coloured dessert generally made with raspberries and redcurrants, though you can easily substitute any other soft fruit in season.

Grease a 1-litre/1¾-pint pudding basin. Place the prepared fruits in a bowl and add the sugar dissolved in the water. Toss gently, taking care not to bruise the fruit. If this is very firm, or if the sugar has not dissolved adequately, then heat very gently so that the fruit juices begin to run. Allow to cool.

Line the bottom and sides of the pudding basin with about 11 of the bread slices, trimming each slice to make a neat fit. Cut the remaining three slices into round discs to fit the basin. Spoon one-third of the fruit into the bottom of the basin and top with a bread disc. Repeat this procedure twice more, finishing with a bread disc. Cover the pudding with a plate and put a heavy weight on top to press the fruit down firmly. Chill in the refrigerator for 8 hours, or long enough for the juices to penetrate and soak the bread.

To serve, turn the pudding out on to a serving dish and serve alone or with fresh cream.

Variation

Autumn pudding: A delicious variation on summer pudding can be made using autumn fruits like peeled and stoned plums, hulled blackberries and peeled, cored and sliced apples or pears. Use equal quantities of the chosen fruits to make up to about 900 g/2 lb. Cook gently together in a little water and the sugar and continue as above.

Peach Melba

SERVES 4

4 peaches
350 g/12 oz sugar
900 ml/1½ pints water
1 vanilla pod or a few drops of vanilla essence
MELBA SAUCE
225 g/8 oz raspberries, hulled
4-5 tablespoons icing sugar, sifted
1 recipe Rich vanilla ice cream (page 98) or
600 ml/1 pint bought vanilla ice cream
chopped nuts to decorate

To loosen the skin, place the peaches in a bowl and pour over boiling water to cover. Drain immediately, leave to cool then using a sharp knife carefully peel away the skin. Cut the peaches in half and remove and discard the stones.

Meanwhile, place the sugar in a saucepan with the water and bring slowly to the boil. Add the peaches and the vanilla, reduce the heat and simmer for 5-10 minutes until cooked but still firm. Remove with a slotted spoon and leave to cool.

Prepare the Melba sauce. Purée the raspberries in an electric blender or pass through a fine nylon sieve. If you use an electric blender, then sieve the purée to remove any seeds. Gradually add the icing sugar, a little at a time, stirring constantly, until a slightly thickened sauce is produced and the sweetening is according to taste. Chill before serving.

To serve, place two peach halves in each serving dish. Top with a large scoop of ice cream. Spoon over the Melba sauce and sprinkle with chopped nuts. Serve at once.

Honey fruit salad

SERVES 6

225 g/8 oz green seedless grapes
225 g/8 oz black grapes, seeds removed
2 oranges, peeled, pith removed and segmented
2 apples, cored and sliced
2 bananas, peeled and sliced
150 ml/¼ pint light red wine
150 ml/¼ pint water
3 tablespoons clear honey
1 tablespoon lemon juice
2 cloves
50 g/2 oz Brazil nuts, halved

Mix all the fruit together in a large serving bowl. In a saucepan, heat together the wine, water, honey, lemon juice and cloves for a few minutes to mix and flavour. Leave to macerate for 15 minutes then remove the cloves. Pour the still-warm liquid over the fruit and leave to cool. Stir in the nuts just before serving.

Bubbling plum and orange compote

25 g/1 oz raisins
100 ml/4 fl oz medium dry sherry
3 tablespoons dark soft brown sugar
1 cinnamon stick
2 large oranges
450 g/1 lb red plums, halved and stoned
soured cream to serve (optional)

Place the raisins, sherry, sugar, cinnamon stick and a strip of orange rind pared from one of the oranges in a saucepan and bring to the boil. Remove from the heat and allow to cool until just lukewarm.

Add the plums to this mixture and cook gently for about 6-8 minutes, or until the plums are tender but still retain their shape. Peel the rind and pith from the oranges and cut the flesh into segments. Add to the plum mixture and heat through. Remove and discard the orange rind and cinnamon stick. Serve the compote hot with soured cream, if liked.

Pineapple, banana and fig flambé

900 g/2 lb firm bananas
1 medium pineapple, peeled, cored and cut into
2.5-cm/1-inch chunks
100 g/4 oz dried figs, cut into strips or 2 large
fresh figs, peeled and chopped
50 g/2 oz butter
100 g/4 oz Demerara sugar
3 tablespoons lemon juice
½ teaspoon mixed spice
25 g/1 oz hazelnuts, chopped
4 tablespoons dark rum

Peel and thickly slice the bananas into a shallow ovenproof dish. Top with the pineapple and figs. Place the butter in a saucepan and heat until melted. Stir in the sugar, lemon juice and spice and heat until well mixed. Pour over the prepared fruits. Cover tightly and cook in a moderately hot oven (200 C, 400 F, Gas Mark 6) for 20-25 minutes. Remove from the oven and sprinkle with the nuts.

Heat the rum in a small saucepan, ignite and pour over the fruit. Serve at once.

Spiced wine pears

4 large firm pears
300 ml/½ pint red wine (claret or Burgundy
for example)
225 g/8 oz sugar
2 cloves
small strip of lemon rind

Peel the pears carefully, leaving the stalks intact. Heat the red wine with the sugar in a large saucepan until it has completely dissolved. Add the pears, cloves and lemon rind and simmer, covered, until just tender, about 20-30 minutes. Baste the pears from time to time with the red wine syrup. When cooked, remove the pears with a slotted spoon and place on a serving dish. Remove and discard the cloves and lemon rind from the syrup.

Reduce the syrup over a high heat to about half its quantity then spoon over the cooked pears and serve hot or cold.

Barnstaple Fair pears

6 large ripe firm pears
75 g/3 oz raisins
75 g/3 oz chopped mixed nuts
2 tablespoons clear honey
175 ml/6 fl oz dry white wine
1½ tablespoons ginger marmalade
150 g/5 oz redcurrant jelly

Grease an ovenproof baking dish large enough to hold six pears. Cut a thin slice from the base of the washed but not peeled pears so that they will stand upright in the dish. Remove a small 'cap' from the top of each pear and reserve. Scoop out and discard the core and pips of the pears using a teaspoon. Mix the raisins, nuts and honey together and use to fill the pears. Place in the dish and replace each pear cap. Pour the wine over the pears and cover lightly with cooking foil. Bake in a moderately hot oven (200 C, 400 F, Gas Mark 6) for 30 minutes.

Lift the pears carefully into individual serving bowls and keep warm. Stir the marmalade and redcurrant jelly into the juices and bring to the boil. Simmer for 5 minutes, until the jelly has completely dissolved. Remove the pear caps, pour the liquid over the pears, replace the caps and serve at once.

The long and short of it

. . . tempting dishes made from rice and pasta

Long-grain, short or round-grain, brown, white or wild, plain, wholemeal or shaped – there's much more to rice and pasta than the plain nursery pudding. Serve it with dried or fresh fruit and a handful of nuts and you have a team that is unbeatable for a wide range of super puddings and desserts.

The secret of good rice and pasta lies in that hint of a bite to the rice grain or pasta dough, so it is important that both should be carefully watched to prevent overcooking. When cooking rice, measure the amount of liquid specified in the following recipes exactly and you can be sure of separated but well-cooked grains. Follow the manufacturer's packet instructions for cooking pasta. You can experiment with some of the more unusual shapes as well as the different types of pasta to give variety without drastically changing the flavour of the dish.

Most of the following rice recipes use short-grain rice but if you'd like something different, then ring the changes by substituting any of the other grains, adjusting the cooking times accordingly, and you'll appreciate the difference. The recipe times for the pasta recipes refer to dried packet pasta, but if you are lucky enough to be able to buy fresh pasta or enjoy making your own, then you can simply substitute it. However, remember to reduce the cooking times slightly and increase the weight – fresh pasta weighs more than dried pasta but produces the same volume.

Creamy rice pudding and Rice and sultana flan (overleaf); Banana pasta dolce (page 58)

Creamy rice pudding

3 tablespoons short-grain rice
600 ml/1 pint milk
1 vanilla pod
25 g/1 oz castor sugar
150 ml/¼ pint double cream

Bring the rice, milk, vanilla pod and sugar to the boil in a saucepan. Either place in the top of a double boiler and cook gently for 1½ hours until tender or place in an ovenproof dish and cook in a cool oven (150 C, 300 F, Gas Mark 2) for about 2 hours. Remove the vanilla pod and allow to cool slightly.

Whip the cream until it stands in soft peaks. Fold the cream into the rice and serve hot or cold.

Variations

Creamy rice and raisin pudding: Prepare the pudding as above. Add 50 g/2 oz raisins to the cooked hot rice pudding and simmer or bake for a further 5 minutes. Sprinkle with a little ground nutmeg if baking the dish. Fold in the whipped cream and serve hot or cold, sprinkled with a few toasted nuts.
Spiced lemon rind rice pudding: Add the finely grated rind of 1 lemon and 1 cinnamon stick about 7.5 cm/3 inches long to the rice before cooking. Cook as above and remove the cinnamon stick before serving.
Banana rice pudding: Slice 2 bananas. At the end of the cooking time arrange the banana slices on top of the rice pudding and sprinkle with 50 g/2 oz soft brown sugar. Place under a preheated grill until the sugar caramelises.
Chilled chocolate rice: Allow the cooked rice pudding to cool completely, then divide it between four individual glass dishes and chill thoroughly. Meanwhile, make the chocolate sauce (page 81) and allow to cool. Swirl a little chocolate sauce through each portion and top with a few toasted chopped hazelnuts. Serve immediately.

Rice and sultana flan

450 ml/¾ pint milk
3 tablespoons short-grain rice
50 g/2 oz sultanas
2 tablespoons Irish coffee cream liqueur
1 tablespoon castor sugar
3 eggs, beaten
CRUMB CRUST
100 g/4 oz digestive biscuits, crushed
50 g/2 oz coconut cookies, crushed
75 g/3 oz butter, melted
150 ml/¼ pint double cream, whipped
candied coffee beans to decorate

Place the milk and rice in a heavy-based saucepan. Bring to the boil and simmer for about 30 minutes or until the rice is tender and most of the milk has been absorbed. Allow to cool.

Meanwhile, soak the sultanas in the liqueur for about 20 minutes and stir into the rice with the sugar and eggs.

To make the crumb crust, mix the biscuit crumbs together and bind with the butter. Use to line a 20-cm/8-inch fluted flan ring standing on a baking tray. Pour in the rice mixture and bake in a moderate oven (180 C, 350 F, Gas Mark 4) for 30-35 minutes or until just set. Allow to cool.

Serve the flan decorated with swirls of whipped cream and candied coffee beans.

Fluffy cherry rice

— SERVES 4 —

75 g/3 oz short-grain rice
600 ml/1 pint milk
2 tablespoons castor sugar
grated rind of ½ lemon
½ teaspoon ground nutmeg
50 g/2 oz raisins
2 eggs, separated
225 g/8 oz red cherries, stoned

Place the rice, milk, sugar, lemon rind and nutmeg in a saucepan and bring to the boil. Reduce the heat and simmer for 15 minutes, stirring from time to time. Stir the raisins and egg yolks into the rice, mixing well.

Whisk the egg whites until they stand in firm peaks and fold into the rice mixture. Place the cherries in the base of a 1-litre/2-pint ovenproof dish and top with the rice mixture. Bake in a moderate oven (180 C, 350 F, Gas Mark 4) for 20-30 minutes, or until golden brown.

Tutti frutti rice

— SERVES 6 —

1.2 litres/2 pints milk
150 g/5 oz castor sugar
75 g/3 oz short-grain rice
1 teaspoon vanilla essence
1 recipe Custard sauce (page 86)
150 ml/¼ pint double cream
2 tablespoons powdered gelatine
50 g/2 oz flaked almonds
25 g/1 oz raisins
2 tablespoons chopped coloured glacé cherries

Place the milk and sugar in a saucepan. Bring to the boil and add the rice. Simmer gently for about 50 minutes or until the rice is tender and has absorbed almost all the milk. Stir in the vanilla essence and allow to cool.

When cool, stir the cooled custard sauce into the rice. Whip the cream until it stands in soft peaks and fold into the custard and rice mixture. Mix the gelatine with 3 tablespoons cold water in a small bowl. Place the bowl in a saucepan of hot water and heat until the gelatine is clear and dissolved. Stir into the rice mixture. Fold in the nuts, raisins and cherries. Pour into a dampened 1.5-litre/ 2½-pint ring mould and chill until set. Turn out on to a serving dish to serve.

Japanese rice balls with sultana sauce

50 g/2 oz short-grain rice
1 small egg, beaten
1 tablespoon brown sugar
75 g/3 oz fresh white breadcrumbs
oil for deep frying
SULTANA SAUCE
150 g/5 oz sultanas
1 tablespoon sugar
2 teaspoons cornflour
100 ml/4 fl oz sweet sherry

In a saucepan, cook the rice in 600 ml/1 pint water or half milk and half water for about 30 minutes or until the rice is tender and all the liquid has been absorbed. Allow to cool and mix in the egg and sugar.

Form the rice mixture into small walnut-sized balls and coat in the breadcrumbs. Heat the oil to 180 C/350 F and fry the rice balls until golden, about 6 minutes. Drain on absorbent kitchen paper.

Meanwhile, prepare the sauce. Place the sultanas in a saucepan with 250 ml/8 fl oz water. Simmer until plump and tender, about 5 minutes. Add the sugar and heat to dissolve. Mix the cornflour with the sherry and mix into the sultana liquid. Bring to the boil, stirring continuously, and simmer for 2-3 minutes. Serve poured over the warm rice balls.

Blackberry and apple condé

600 ml/1 pint milk
75 g/3 oz short-grain rice
25 g/1 oz castor sugar
150 ml/¼ pint single cream
450 g/1 lb dessert apples, peeled, cored
and sliced
225 g/8 oz blackberries, hulled
25 g/1 oz butter
3 tablespoons soft brown sugar
150 ml/¼ pint double cream

Heat the milk with the rice and castor sugar in a saucepan until boiling. Place in an ovenproof casserole, cover and cook in a cool oven (150 C, 300 F, Gas Mark 2) for 1 hour, or until the rice is tender. Cool, then stir in 4 tablespoons of the single cream. Spoon into a 1.5-litre/2½-pint serving dish.

In a saucepan, cook the sliced apple in about 2 tablespoons water until just tender, about 5 minutes. Add the blackberries, butter and sugar and cook for a further 2-3 minutes. Cool, then spoon over the rice.

Whip the remaining single cream with the double cream until it stands in soft peaks. Pipe or spoon over the blackberry and apple mixture. Chill lightly before serving.

Moulded gooseberry condé

SERVES 6

3 tablespoons short-grain rice
600 ml/1 pint milk
10 tablespoons gooseberry jam
1 (298-g/10½-oz) can gooseberries
2 teaspoons powdered gelatine
150 ml/¼ pint double cream
2 teaspoons arrowroot
1 tablespoon lemon juice
mint leaves to decorate (optional)

Place the rice and milk in a heavy-based saucepan and bring to the boil. Simmer until the rice is tender, about 35 minutes. Stir in 2 tablespoons of the jam and allow to cool.

Drain the canned gooseberries, reserving the juice, and fold the fruit into the cooled rice. Place the gelatine in a small bowl and place the bowl in a saucepan of hot water. Heat until the gelatine dissolves and becomes clear. Stir into the rice mixture. Whip the cream until it stands in soft peaks and fold into the rice mixture. Turn into a lightly oiled 1-litre/1¾-pint fluted ring mould. Chill to set.

Heat the remaining jam in a saucepan with 6 tablespoons of the reserved gooseberry juice and the arrowroot. Bring to the boil to thicken. Stir in the lemon juice and cool.

To serve, turn out the rice condé on to a serving plate and spoon over some of the sauce. Serve the remaining sauce separately. Decorate the condé with mint leaves, if liked.

Natural health semolina or sago pudding

SERVES 4

600 ml/1 pint milk
40 g/1½ oz natural or wholemeal semolina
or sago
25 g/1 oz Demerara sugar
½ teaspoon mixed spice
50 g/2 oz raisins
50 g/2 oz chopped mixed nuts

Scald the milk in a saucepan. Sprinkle in the semolina or sago and bring slowly to the boil. Cook for 3-4 minutes, stirring, until the mixture thickens.

Add the sugar, spice and raisins, mixing well. Continue to cook for about 7-8 minutes, stirring constantly. Turn into individual bowls and top with the chopped nuts. Serve at once.

Variation

Natural health semolina or sago pudding with fruit: This pudding is doubly delicious if served over poached or stewed fruit like apples, plums, damsons, greengages or gooseberries. Allow 450 g/1 lb stewed or poached fruit for 4 servings.

Lokshen pudding

225 g/8 oz vermicelli
50 g/2 oz butter
50 g/2 oz sultanas
50 g/2 oz chopped mixed peel
50 g/2 oz slivered almonds
2 eggs
pinch of ground nutmeg
pinch of ground cinnamon
50 g/2 oz castor sugar
300 ml/½ pint double cream (optional)

In a saucepan, cook the vermicelli in boiling water following the packet instructions, about 6 minutes. Drain and return to the saucepan with the butter. Toss the pasta in the butter to coat evenly. Add the sultanas, the mixed peel and half the almonds and mix well. Beat the eggs with the nutmeg and cinnamon. Stir in the sugar. Pour into the pasta mixture and mix well.

Turn into an ovenproof dish and sprinkle with the remaining nuts. Bake in a moderate oven (180 C, 350 F, Gas Mark 4) for 10-15 minutes or until lightly set. Brown quickly under a hot grill until golden and serve with the unwhipped double cream, if liked.

Banana pasta dolce

225 g/8 oz broken macaroni
750 ml/1¼ pints milk
40 g/1½ oz castor sugar
40 g/1½ oz Demerara sugar
¼ teaspoon ground nutmeg
¼ teaspoon ground cinnamon
4 ripe bananas, peeled and sliced
3 tablespoons chopped mixed nuts

Place the macaroni in a saucepan or flameproof gratin dish with the milk. Bring to the boil and simmer for 6 minutes. Add the sugars and cook, stirring, for a further 10 minutes. Add the spices and banana, toss and either turn into a serving dish or serve in the pan. Sprinkle with the nuts and serve at once.

Variation

Peach pasta dolce: Prepare as above but use 1 (398-g/14-oz) can peach slices instead of the bananas. Drain from their syrup before tossing in the pasta mixture.

Macaroni applecake

175 g/6 oz ginger nut or digestive biscuits,
crushed
75 g/3 oz butter, melted
2 (425-g/15-oz) cans creamed macaroni
grated rind and juice of 1 lemon
2 dessert apples, peeled, cored and grated
$\frac{1}{2}$ teaspoon mixed spice
50 g/2 oz castor sugar
150 ml/$\frac{1}{4}$ pint whipped cream
1 red-skinned apple, cored and thinly sliced

Mix the biscuit crumbs with the melted butter in a bowl.
Combine the creamed macaroni with the lemon rind,
grated apple, mixed spice and sugar. Put half the creamed
macaroni mixture into a glass bowl. Cover with most of
the crumb mixture and then the remaining macaroni.
Sprinkle with the remaining crumb mixture and pipe or
spoon the whipped cream over the mixture. Chill for at
least 30 minutes.

Serve the applecake decorated with apple slices dipped
in lemon juice to prevent discoloration.

Orange macaroni pudding

50 g/2 oz broken macaroni
600 ml/1 pint milk, warmed
25 g/1 oz castor sugar
2 teaspoons finely grated orange rind
1 strip of lemon rind
ground nutmeg (optional)
15 g/$\frac{1}{2}$ oz butter
orange rind to decorate

Place the macaroni in a 900-ml/1$\frac{1}{2}$-pint greased ovenproof
dish and add the milk. Leave to soften for 30 minutes.

Add the sugar, orange and lemon rind and mix well.
Sprinkle the top with nutmeg, if used, and dot with the
butter. Bake in a cool oven (150 C, 300 F, Gas Mark 2) for
2-2$\frac{1}{2}$ hours, stirring twice during the first hour of cooking.
Remove the strip of lemon rind and serve, decorated with
a twist of orange rind.

Out of this world

. . . light-as-air recipes for soufflés and meringues

Surely ranked the lightest of desserts, soufflés and meringues are the airy and flamboyant opposites of the heavier image that is often associated with the term 'pudding'. Yet they have little in common with each other apart from the basic egg. The meringue can be fluffy or crisp and lends itself to simple presentation as well as elaborate assembly, while the soufflé cannot really be anything other than grand with its basic components of cream, eggs, fruit purées or chocolate, coffee and praline flavourings, to mention just a few.

They are both equally delicious, however, served either hot or cold. A hot, magnificently risen sweet soufflé is just as tempting as a warm baked lemon meringue pie and a cool, cream-filled vacherin is an admirable match for any elegant cold fruit soufflé.

However sophisticated you consider soufflés or meringues, some of the classics or favourites have surprisingly humble beginnings. For instance, Queen of puddings, Apple amber and Floating islands were all developed to use up leftovers.

Make any of the following recipes part of your repertoire of dishes and you are sure to receive some hearty compliments.

Strawberry soufflé and Hot mocha soufflé (overleaf); Raspberry meringue nests (page 66)

Classic lemon soufflé

3 eggs, separated
75 g/3 oz castor sugar
grated rind and juice of 2 lemons
15 g/½ oz powdered gelatine
150 ml/¼ pint double cream
100 g/4 oz chopped nuts
100 ml/4 fl oz double cream, whipped
lemon slices to decorate

Lightly grease a 600-ml/1-pint soufflé dish. Cut a double strip of greaseproof paper, equal in width to the height of the dish plus 5 cm/2 inches and long enough to go right round the outside of the dish. Lightly grease the top 5 cm/ 2 inches and tie securely with string around the outside of the dish, greased side inside (see page 120).

Place the egg yolks and sugar in a bowl over a saucepan of simmering water and whisk together until thick and creamy. Add the lemon rind and juice. Put the gelatine in a small bowl with 3 tablespoons water. Put the bowl in a saucepan of hot water and leave until the gelatine is clear and dissolved, stirring occasionally.

Whisk the egg whites until they stand in soft peaks and whip the cream until stiff. Stir the gelatine into the lemon mixture, then fold in the cream and finally the egg white. Pour gently into the prepared soufflé dish, levelling off the top, and chill until set.

Before serving, carefully ease the greaseproof paper away from the soufflé using the back of a knife. Press chopped nuts around the sides of the soufflé. Decorate the top with swirls of whipped cream and slices of lemon.

Variations

Still considered by many to be the most stunning of desserts, Lemon soufflé is really simple to prepare and with a little imagination can be transformed into many delicious variations.

Strawberry soufflé: Follow the recipe for Lemon soufflé but use 150 ml/¼ pint strawberry purée instead of the two lemons. Decorate with whipped cream and sliced strawberries.

Orange soufflé: Follow the recipe for Lemon soufflé but use the grated rind and juice of 1 large orange plus 1 tablespoon lemon juice in place of the 2 lemons. For special occasions, add 1 tablespoon Grand Marnier or Cointreau. Decorate with chopped nuts, whipped cream and orange slices.

Chocolate Barbados soufflé: Follow the recipe for Lemon soufflé but use 75 g/3 oz chocolate melted in 2 tablespoons milk instead of the 2 lemons. For special occasions, add 1 tablespoon dark rum. Use toasted coconut to coat the sides of the soufflé in place of chopped nuts. Decorate with whipped cream and chocolate curls.

Coffee praline soufflé: Follow the recipe for Lemon soufflé but use 150 ml/¼ pint strong black coffee in place of the 2 lemons and add 2 tablespoons crushed praline or caramel. For special occasions, add 1 tablespoon Tia Maria. Decorate with chopped nuts, whipped cream and candied coffee beans.

Hot mocha soufflé with Tia Maria cream

SOUFFLÉ
100 g/4 oz plain chocolate
4 tablespoons strong black coffee
40 g/1½ oz butter
40 g/1½ oz plain flour
225 ml/8 fl oz milk
50 g/2 oz castor sugar
2-3 drops vanilla essence
3 egg yolks
4 egg whites
1 tablespoon Tia Maria
2 tablespoons icing sugar, sifted
TIA MARIA CREAM
150 ml/¼ pint single cream
2 tablespoons Tia Maria

Prepare a 15-cm/6-inch soufflé dish by cutting a double-thickness band of greaseproof paper that is long enough to wrap around the dish and overlap by about 5 cm/2 inches, and wide enough to stand 7.5 cm/3 inches above it. Grease the inside of the dish and the top, inside part of the greaseproof paper. Wrap around the outside of the dish and secure with string (see page 120).

To make the soufflé, break the chocolate into small pieces and place in a small bowl with the coffee. Place the bowl over a saucepan of boiling water and allow to melt, stirring occasionally. Melt the butter in a saucepan, add the flour and cook for 1-2 minutes. Gradually add the milk, stirring continuously, to make a smooth, thick sauce. Add the sugar and vanilla essence and mix well. Remove the pan from the heat and stir in the coffee and chocolate mixture. Allow to cool slightly, then beat in the egg yolks. Whisk the egg whites until they stand in firm peaks, then using a metal spoon, fold carefully into the chocolate mixture, taking care not to lose much air. Finally fold in the Tia Maria. Pour into the prepared soufflé dish and make a small 'trough' around the edge of the soufflé with a teaspoon, about 2.5 cm/1 inch from the rim of the dish and about 1 cm/½ inch deep. This will help the soufflé to rise and give it a distinctive 'crown'.

Bake on the centre shelf of a moderately hot oven (190 C, 375 F, Gas Mark 5) for 25 minutes. Carefully sprinkle the top of the soufflé with the icing sugar while still in the oven, then continue to bake for a further 5 minutes.

Meanwhile, to make the Tia Maria cream, mix the single cream with the Tia Maria. Serve the soufflé *immediately* with the Tia Maria cream. Do not remove the paper collar until serving at the table since any cold air or draught can cause the soufflé to collapse in seconds rather than minutes.

Little orange soufflés

SERVES 4

4 large oranges
4 eggs, separated
50 g/2 oz castor sugar
1 tablespoon Cointreau, Grand Marnier or
frozen concentrated orange juice, thawed
1 tablespoon icing sugar, sifted

Carefully slice the tops from the oranges and scoop out the flesh. Reserve the shells and zig-zag the top edge for decoration, if liked. Remove the rind from the caps of the oranges and cut into very thin julienne strips. Cook the orange strips in a little boiling water for 5 minutes to soften. Drain and cool. Extract the juice from the orange flesh and place the juice in a saucepan. Bring to the boil and reduce until just 1 tablespoon orange juice remains.

Place the egg yolks and sugar in a bowl and whisk until very thick and creamy. Add the orange rind, warm orange juice and Cointreau, Grand Marnier or concentrated orange juice. In another bowl, whisk the egg whites until they stand in firm peaks. Fold into the orange mixture using a metal spoon. Spoon equal quantities of the soufflé mixture into each orange case. Place on a baking tray and bake in a hot oven (230 C, 450 F, Gas Mark 8) for 10 minutes. While the oranges are still in the oven, sprinkle the tops with the icing sugar. Bake for a further 2-3 minutes, then serve at once.

Ginger soufflé

SERVES 6

4 eggs, separated
75 g/3 oz Demerara sugar
½ teaspoon ground ginger
450 ml/¾ pint milk
1 tablespoon powdered gelatine
6 tablespoons ginger wine
150 ml/¼ pint soured cream
25 g/1 oz stem ginger, finely chopped
300 ml/½ pint double cream, whipped
crystallised stem ginger and chopped almonds
to decorate

Prepare a 15-cm/6-inch large soufflé dish or six 150-ml/ ¼-pint soufflé dishes by tying a double-thickness band of greaseproof paper around the dish, extended 5 cm/2 inches above the rim (page 120). Grease both dish and top.

Whisk the egg yolks, sugar and ginger together in a bowl. Scald the milk in a saucepan and pour on to the egg mixture, whisking constantly. Return to the saucepan and heat, stirring, until the custard thickens and lightly coats the back of the spoon. *Do not allow to boil.* Mix the gelatine with 3 tablespoons of water in a bowl and stand the bowl in a saucepan of hot water until the gelatine has dissolved. Stir into the cooled custard with the ginger wine. Chill until almost set then stir in the soured cream and stem ginger. Fold in half the whipped cream. Whisk the egg whites until stiff and fold into the custard. Pour into the prepared soufflé dish and chill until set.

To serve, remove the collar, decorate with the remaining cream, stem ginger and chopped almonds.

Frozen ice cream soufflé

— SERVES 6 —

6 egg yolks
175 g/6 oz castor sugar
1-2 drops of vanilla essence
600 ml/1 pint double cream, whipped
225 g/8 oz fresh strawberries, hulled
1 tablespoon icing sugar, sifted (optional)
4 tablespoons strong black coffee
4 tablespoons roasted hazelnuts, chopped
150 ml/¼ pint double cream, whipped
fresh strawberries and chocolate curls
to decorate

Place the egg yolks, castor sugar and vanilla essence in a bowl over a saucepan of simmering water. Whisk until thick and creamy. Remove from the heat and whisk until cool. Fold in the 600 ml/1 pint whipped cream and divide this ice cream base into three portions.

Purée the strawberries, sieve and sweeten with the icing sugar if necessary. Add this purée to one portion of the ice cream base, mixing well. Add the coffee and hazelnuts to the second ice cream base, mixing well, leaving the third ice cream base plain.

Tie a double-thickness band of greaseproof paper around the outside of a 15-cm/6-inch soufflé dish so that it extends 7.5 cm/3 inches above the rim and secure with string (see page 120). Place half of the plain ice cream mixture into the base of the dish and freeze until firm. Top with half the coffee mixture and freeze until firm. Top again with half the strawberry mixture and freeze until firm. Repeat the last three layers once more. Freeze the whole soufflé until firm, about 3-6 hours.

To serve, remove the greaseproof paper, decorate with whipped cream, fresh strawberries and chocolate curls.

Blackberry or blackcurrant meringue ring

— SERVES 6 —

225 g/8 oz blackcurrants, topped and tailed,
or blackberries
2 tablespoons icing sugar, sifted
2 tablespoons sweet sherry
150 ml/¼ pint double cream
150 ml/¼ pint whipping cream
12 meringue shells (page 71)
150 ml/¼ pint double cream, whipped and
fresh blackcurrants or blackberries to decorate

Place the blackcurrants or blackberries in a bowl with the icing sugar and sherry and leave to macerate for at least 2 hours. Purée this mixture in an electric blender, then pass through a fine nylon sieve. Whip the double and whipping creams together until they form soft peaks. Break up the meringue shells into small pieces and fold through the cream. Finally, gently fold the fruit purée through the cream to give a marbled effect. Spoon into an 18-cm/7-inch springform tin with fluted base. Cover with cooking foil and freeze until firm, about 4 hours.

To serve, turn out the ring on to a serving dish and decorate the base with the whipped cream and fresh blackcurrants or blackberries. Allow to stand in the refrigerator for 15-30 minutes to soften slightly before serving.

64

Fruit Pavlova

MERINGUE BASE
3 egg whites
175 g/6 oz castor sugar
1 teaspoon cornflour
$\frac{1}{4}$ teaspoon vanilla essence
1 teaspoon lemon juice
FILLING
300 ml/$\frac{1}{2}$ pint whipping or double cream
450 g/1 lb mixed prepared fresh fruits
(for example, strawberries, raspberries, orange
segments, sliced kiwi fruit, halved grapes,
passion fruit and sliced peaches)

Mark an 18-cm/7-inch circle on a piece of rice paper or greased greaseproof paper. Place the paper on a baking tray.

Whisk the egg whites until they stand in stiff peaks. Whisk in half the sugar, a little at a time, beating well until the meringue is thick and glossy and stands in firm peaks (see page 120). Sift the remaining sugar with the cornflour then fold into the meringue with the vanilla essence and lemon juice.

Spoon or pipe the meringue on to the paper, following the line of the circle and covering the base but making a hollow in the centre of the meringue to hold the fruit later. Bake in the centre of a cool oven (150 C, 300 F, Gas Mark 2) for 1$\frac{1}{4}$-1$\frac{1}{2}$ hours until firm and lightly coloured. Cool, then remove the paper.

For the filling, whip the cream until it stands in soft peaks, then pile into the centre of the pavlova. Top with the prepared fruit and chill lightly before serving.

Queen of puddings

300 ml/$\frac{1}{2}$ pint milk
100 g/4 oz castor sugar
3 eggs, separated
75 g/3 oz soft white breadcrumbs
3 tablespoons strawberry jam
1 tablespoon lemon juice
fresh or glacé cherries and toasted
flaked almonds to decorate

Grease a medium-size pie dish. Whisk the milk, 25 g/1 oz of the castor sugar and the egg yolks together. Pour over the breadcrumbs in a mixing bowl and leave to soak for 15 minutes. Mix the jam and lemon juice together. Put the softened crumbs and milk mixture into the pie dish and bake in a moderate oven (180 C, 350 F, Gas Mark 4) for 20 minutes. Remove from the oven and spread with the jam mixture.

Whisk the egg whites until they stand in stiff peaks, then gradually whisk in the remaining sugar, 1 tablespoon at a time, until the meringue is stiff and glossy. Pipe or spoon over the pudding. Dust with a little extra castor sugar, if liked, and bake for a further 15 minutes or until the meringue is set and golden. Decorate with fresh or glacé cherries and toasted flaked almonds.

Raspberry meringue nest

— SERVES 4-6 —

MERINGUE NEST
4 egg whites
250 g/9 oz icing sugar, sifted
1 teaspoon vanilla essence
FILLING
1 small pineapple, peeled, cored and cut
into chunks
3 tablespoons Kirsch (optional)
350 g/12 oz fresh raspberries, hulled
2-3 tablespoons icing sugar, sifted (optional)
600 ml/1 pint ice cream, flavour according
to taste

Line a baking tray with rice paper or greased greaseproof paper. Mark a 20-cm/8-inch circle on the paper if you wish to make one large meringue nest. Alternatively, mark 4 (7.5-cm/3-inch) circles for four small nests. Place the egg whites in a bowl and place the bowl over a saucepan of simmering water. Gradually add the icing sugar, whisking constantly until the meringue stands in firm peaks. Add the vanilla essence and mix well. Using a piping bag fitted with a star-shaped nozzle, fill with the meringue mixture. To make the large nest and using the marked circle as a guideline, pipe a continuous circle of meringue, working from the outside to the centre of the circle to form the base of the nest. To create a decorative wall, pipe one row of individual rosettes around the edge of the base, and repeat with a second row of rosettes on top. If making the small nests, pipe a base of meringue as above and pipe another circle around the edge to form a nest. Place in a very cool oven (110 C, 225 F, Gas Mark ¼) and bake for 4-5 hours or leave overnight. Cool and remove any paper.

Meanwhile, soak the pineapple chunks in the Kirsch, if used. Purée 225 g/8 oz of the raspberries in an electric blender, pass through a fine sieve to remove any pips and sweeten, if liked, with icing sugar.

To serve the meringue nest, fill the centre with ice cream. Add the remaining raspberries and pineapple and top with the raspberry purée.

Baked Alaska

— SERVES 6 —

SPONGE BASE
150 g/5 oz plain flour, sifted
100 g/4 oz castor sugar
1½ teaspoons baking powder
½ teaspoon salt
50 g/2 oz butter or margarine
100 ml/4 fl oz milk
1 egg
1 teaspoon vanilla essence
or **1 round, ready-prepared sponge cake,**
measuring 20 cm/8 inches in diameter
FILLING
2 tablespoons dark rum (optional)
1 (1-litre/35.2-fl oz) carton ice cream
(for example, raspberry ripple, chocolate or
Neapolitan)
MERINGUE TOPPING
3 egg whites
150 g/5 oz castor sugar

Grease and flour a 23-cm/9-inch square cake tin. Sift the flour, sugar, baking powder and salt into a bowl. Add the butter or margarine and milk and beat, with an electric whisk or spoon, until thick and well blended. Add the egg and vanilla essence and beat for a further 2 minutes. Pour the mixture into the cake tin and bake in a moderate oven (180 C, 350 F, Gas Mark 4) for 20-25 minutes, or until the cake springs back when lightly pressed in the centre. Cool on a wire rack.

Meanwhile, if using a round sponge cake, shape the ice cream brick into a round on a piece of cooking foil to the same size as the cake. Freeze to harden again.

Place the cooled cake on a cutting board. Trim two 5-cm/2-inch wide strips from each side of the cake to match the shape of an ice-cream brick. (Reserve these and use for trifle sponges.) Sprinkle the rum over the cake, if used. To prepare the meringue topping, whisk the egg whites until they form stiff peaks. Gradually whisk in half the sugar and continue beating until the mixture is thick and glossy. Fold in the remaining sugar with a metal spoon.

Place the ice cream on the sponge. Spoon or pipe the meringue on to the ice cream and sponge to cover it completely. Bake in a hot oven (230 C, 450 F, Gas Mark 8) for 3-5 minutes or until the meringue is tinged golden. Serve at once.

Lemon meringue pie

SERVES 4-6

RICH SHORTCRUST PASTRY
175 g/6 oz plain flour
pinch of salt
125 g/4½ oz butter or margarine
1 egg yolk
1-2 tablespoons iced water
LEMON FILLING
3 tablespoons cornflour
300 ml/½ pint milk
50 g/2 oz castor sugar
pinch of salt
3 egg yolks
grated rind and juice of 2 lemons
MERINGUE TOPPING
2 egg whites
100 g/4 oz castor sugar

First prepare the pastry by sifting the flour and salt into a bowl. Add the butter, cut into small pieces, and rub in with the fingertips until the mixture resembles fine breadcrumbs. Add the egg yolk and 1 tablespoon of the iced water and mix into a firm dough. Add the extra tablespoon of water if necessary. Chill for 30 minutes in the refrigerator.

Roll the pastry out on a lightly floured board or work surface to form a circle large enough to line a 20-cm/8-inch fluted flan ring. Place the flan ring on a greased baking tray and ease the pastry into the flan. Trim away any excess pastry, then bake 'blind' (see page 119) in a hot oven (220 C, 425 F, Gas Mark 7) for 15 minutes. Remove the cooking foil or paper and beans and bake for a further 10 minutes or until the pastry is cooked and golden. Reduce the oven temperature to moderate (160 C, 325 F, Gas Mark 3). Cool the flan on a wire rack.

Prepare the lemon filling by mixing the cornflour with the milk, sugar and salt in a saucepan. Gradually bring to the boil, stirring, and cook for 2 minutes. Remove from the heat and allow to cool slightly then whisk the egg yolks into the milk mixture. Stir in the lemon rind and juice. Cool the mixture for about 20 minutes, then pour into the cooked flan case. Leave to cool.

Meanwhile, for the topping, whisk the egg whites until they stand in stiff peaks. Gradually whisk in the sugar, reserving 1 tablespoon, until the mixture is thick and glossy. Spoon or pipe the meringue on to the lemon pie filling, ensuring that the meringue completely covers the filling. Sprinkle with the remaining castor sugar then bake for 20-25 minutes until the meringue is cooked and tinged golden. Remove the flan ring and serve cold.

Hazelnut meringue gâteau

SERVES 6-8

MERINGUE
6 egg whites
350 g/12 oz castor sugar
2 teaspoons lemon juice
175 g/6 oz ground hazelnuts
25 g/1 oz hazelnuts, finely chopped
FILLING
100 g/4 oz plain chocolate
150 ml/¼ pint soured cream
150 ml/¼ pint double cream, whipped
1 tablespoon brandy
chopped mixed nuts and chocolate curls
to decorate

Line three baking trays with rice paper or greased greaseproof paper and mark a 20-cm/8-inch circle on each.

Whisk the egg whites until they stand in stiff peaks. Gradually add half the sugar and the lemon juice, whisking constantly until thick and glossy (see page 120). Fold in the remaining sugar and the ground hazelnuts, using a metal spoon.

Spread equal amounts of the meringue over the three marked circles and sprinkle one, to form the top, with the chopped hazelnuts. Bake in a very cool oven (110 C, 225 F, Gas Mark ¼) for 2½-3 hours or until the meringue is crisp and dry. Change the meringues around during cooking to ensure even results. Allow to cool on a wire rack, then remove any paper.

To make the filling, break the chocolate into small pieces and place in a bowl over a saucepan of simmering water. When melted, remove from the heat and stir in the soured cream. Finally fold in the whipped cream and brandy. Chill lightly.

Pipe or spoon the filling on to the bottom and middle meringue layers, reserving a little for the top, and sandwich the whole gâteau together. Decorate the top with swirls of the reserved cream, the chopped nuts and chocolate curls. Allow to stand for 1 hour before serving to ensure neat portions when cutting.

Variation

Walnut meringue gâteau: Prepare as above but use 25 g/1 oz finely chopped walnuts instead of the hazelnuts.

Banana peach vacherin

SERVES 6

VACHERIN
3 egg whites
175 g/6 oz castor sugar
75 g/3 oz ground walnuts
FILLING
2 peaches
1 tablespoon icing sugar
2 bananas, peeled, sliced and tossed
in 1 tablespoon lemon juice
300 ml/½ pint double cream, whipped

Line two baking trays with rice paper or greased greaseproof paper and mark a 20-cm/8-inch circle on each. Mark one circle into six segments.

Prepare the vacherin by whisking the egg whites until stiff. Gradually beat in the sugar and whisk until thick and glossy. Fold in the ground walnuts. Fit a piping bag with a 1-cm/½-inch plain nozzle and fill the bag with the meringue mixture. Using the outside rim of the circle as a guide, pipe concentric circles of meringue towards the centre of the full round. Pipe the remaining meringue to form six wedge shapes, each separate, following the lines on the second marked circle. In both cases, allow room for the meringue to spread slightly. Bake in a moderately hot oven (190 C, 375 F, Gas Mark 5) for 30-40 minutes, or until crisp.

Fill the vacherin at least 1 hour before serving to ensure neat portioning of the wedges. Peel and slice one of the peaches. Fold the icing sugar, bananas – reserving a few slices – and the sliced peach into the whipped cream and pile on to the meringue base. Top with the six meringue wedges positioned in the cream at an angle. Decorate with the remaining unpeeled but sliced peach and the banana slices.

Apple amber

SERVES 4-6

675 g/1½ lb cooking apples, peeled,
cored and chopped
2-4 tablespoons sugar, according to taste
grated rind and juice of ½ lemon
25 g/1 oz butter
2 eggs, separated
½ recipe Rich shortcrust pastry (page 68)
50 g/2 oz castor sugar
apple slices, dipped in lemon juice, to decorate

Place the apple, sugar, lemon rind and juice, butter and 1-2 tablespoons of water in a saucepan. Cover and cook until the apple forms a soft purée. Cool slightly then beat in the egg yolks.

Roll out the pastry on a lightly floured board or work surface to form a circle large enough to line a 20-cm/8-inch pie dish. Cut a strip of pastry and place around the rim of the dish. Dampen with water and ease the circle of pastry into the pie dish, pressing the two edges of pastry together firmly. Cut away any excess pastry and use the trimmings to make small pastry shapes to secure along the rim of the pie dish. Pour the apple mixture into the dish and bake in a moderate oven (180 C, 350 F, Gas Mark 4) for 20-25 minutes, or until the pastry is golden and the apple mixture has set. Reduce the oven temperature to cool (150 C, 300 F, Gas Mark 2).

Whisk the egg whites until they stand in stiff peaks. Gradually whisk in all but 1 tablespoon of the sugar until the mixture is thick and glossy. Spoon or pipe the meringue over the apple filling and dust with the remaining sugar. Bake for 30 minutes or until the meringue is golden and crisp. Serve hot, decorated with slices of apple.

Floating islands

———— SERVES 4 ————

CUSTARD
6 egg yolks
75 g/3 oz castor sugar
½ teaspoon vanilla essence
600 ml/1 pint milk
3 tablespoons single cream
MERINGUE ISLANDS
6 egg whites
pinch of salt
75 g/3 oz castor sugar
banana slices dipped in lemon juice, to decorate
(optional)

First prepare the custard by whisking the egg yolks, castor sugar and vanilla essence in a bowl until thick and creamy. Meanwhile, in a saucepan, scald the milk then gradually pour over the egg mixture, beating constantly. Pour into the top saucepan of a double boiler or place the bowl over a saucepan of simmering water and cook, stirring continuously, until the custard thickens and coats the back of a spoon – this can take up to 25 minutes. Stir in the cream, allow to cool, pour into a serving dish and chill.

To make the meringue islands, bring a large pan of boiling water to a slow simmer. Whisk the egg whites and salt together until they stand in firm peaks. Add three-quarters of the sugar and whisk until firm and glossy. Fold in the remaining sugar, using a metal spoon. Drop round tablespoons of the mixture into the simmering water and poach the 'islands' for 2 minutes on each side. Remove with a slotted spoon and drain on absorbent kitchen paper. When well drained, float the islands on top of the chilled custard and serve with slices of banana, if liked.

Nectarine meringues Chantilly

———— MAKES 6 ————

MERINGUES
4 egg whites
250 g/9 oz castor sugar
pink food colouring or coffee essence (optional)
CRÈME CHANTILLY
300 ml/½ pint double cream
2 teaspoons castor sugar
½ teaspoon vanilla essence
2 ripe nectarines, sliced

Line two baking trays with rice paper or greased greaseproof paper. Place the egg whites in a bowl and whisk until they stand in stiff peaks. Gradually whisk in half the sugar, beating until the meringue is thick and glossy. Fold in all but 1 tablespoon of the remaining sugar, using a metal spoon (see page 120). The meringues may be left plain, coloured pink or flavoured with coffee essence at this stage.

Spoon or pipe the meringue into twelve mounds or swirls on the lined baking tray. Sprinkle with the remaining sugar and bake in a cool oven (140 C, 275 F, Gas Mark 1) for 1 hour or until firm and lightly beige in colour (if not flavoured), changing the trays around halfway through baking to ensure even results.

Remove from the oven and turn the meringues over, using a palette knife. Gently press the soft centres of each meringue to make a shallow hollow for the Crème Chantilly. Bake for a further 30 minutes. Allow to cool completely on a wire rack.

Prepare the Crème Chantilly by whipping the cream until thick. Add the sugar and vanilla essence and sandwich together pairs of the meringues with the Chantilly cream and sliced nectarines.

All wrapped up

*. . . simply scrumptious pastries, pies,
cheesecakes, flans and tarts*

Nothing seems more beguiling than a
sugar-crusted, fruit-filled pie – nothing
until you take a look at a luxurious flaky
mille feuilles, a creamy cheesecake, a
nutmeg-dusted custard tart or a rich
chocolate flan. The choice of fillings can be
as overwhelming as the variety of pastries
themselves, not to mention the host of
possible toppings for an assortment of
tasty desserts.

The secret of a good pastry, pie, flan or
tart often lies in the pastry, whether it be
shortcrust, flaky, rough puff, puff or
choux. For best results, prepare the dough
in cool conditions, using chilled water for
all but the choux, and if there is time,
refrigerate the dough and leave it to rest
while you are making the filling.

Fill pastries, pies, flans and tarts or top a
cheesecake with fruit in season; or use
storecupboard ingredients such as chocolate, nuts, jam, syrup and dried fruit for a
variety of fillings and you have the
makings of an expansible repertoire of
what are sure to become family favourites.

Most of the desserts in this section have
the advantage of being suitable for making
in advance and storing in the freezer ready
for the ideal occasion. Remember that
many pies, flans and tarts are all the more
tasty when quickly reheated just before
serving. If chilling flans, cheesecakes and
tarts a long time before eating, then cover
with cling film to keep them fresh and
allow them to stand at room temperature
for about 1 hour before serving.

Clockwise from the top: *Apple and pear
dumplings (page 76); Strawberry palmiers
(page 81); Black bottom pie and Double crust apple
and blackberry pie (overleaf)*

Double crust apple pie

SHORTCRUST PASTRY
275 g/10 oz plain flour
pinch of salt
60 g/2½ oz lard
60 g/2½ oz butter or margarine
3-4 tablespoons cold water
FILLING
900 g/2 lb cooking apples, peeled,
cored and sliced
100 g/4 oz soft light brown sugar
2 tablespoons cornflour
15 g/½ oz preserved ginger, chopped
milk or beaten egg to glaze
castor sugar to sprinkle

Lightly grease the base and sides of a 25-cm/10-inch pie dish. Prepare the pastry by mixing the flour with the salt. Rub in the lard and butter or margarine until the mixture resembles fine breadcrumbs. Add the water and mix to a firm dough. Roll out two-thirds of the pastry on a lightly floured board or work surface to a circle large enough to line the base and sides of the shallow pie dish. Ease the pastry into the dish and trim away any excess pastry. Roll out the trimmings and remaining pastry to form a round large enough to top the filled pie.

For the filling, place half the apples in the pie dish. Mix the sugar and cornflour together and sprinkle half this mixture over the fruit. Sprinkle with the ginger and top with the remaining fruit and cornflour mixture. Brush the rim of the dish with milk or beaten egg and carefully lift the pastry lid on to the pie. Trim away any excess pastry and seal the edges. Flute the pastry rim (see page 121) and make a small hole in the top of the pie for any steam to escape. (A pie funnel may be placed in the centre of the pie to hold up the crust during cooking.) Glaze the pie with milk or beaten egg and sprinkle with castor sugar. Decorate the pie top with any pastry trimmings, if liked.

Bake in a hot oven (220 C, 425 F, Gas Mark 7) on a baking sheet for 30-40 minutes or until golden brown and cooked through. Serve hot or cold with whipped cream.

Variations

Double crust apple and blackberry pie: Follow the recipe above but use 450 g/1 lb hulled blackberries and 450 g/1 lb sliced apples instead of the cooking apples and omit the ginger.
Double crust rhubarb and ginger pie: Follow the recipe above but use 900 g/2 lb sliced rhubarb instead of the cooking apples.
Double crust plum and orange pie: Follow the recipe above but use 900 g/2 lb halved and stoned plums with the grated rind of 1 orange instead of the cooking apples and omit the ginger.

Black bottom pie

RICH SHORTCRUST PASTRY
175 g/6 oz plain flour
pinch of salt
100 g/4 oz butter
2-3 teaspoons cold water
FILLING
450 ml/¾ pint milk
25 g/1 oz cornflour
100 g/4 oz castor sugar
1 egg, separated
7 g/¼ oz powdered gelatine
3 tablespoons hot water
75 g/3 oz plain chocolate, melted
3 tablespoons frozen concentrated orange juice,
thawed
150 ml/¼ pint whipped cream to decorate

This attractive pie is so called because of its chocolate custard base which is topped with a layer of orange custard. First, prepare the pastry by sifting the flour and salt into a bowl. Add the butter. Cut into the flour with a knife, then rub in with the fingertips until the mixture resembles fine breadcrumbs. Sprinkle the water over the crumbs and mix to a firm dough. Roll out on a lightly floured board or work surface to form a circle large enough to line a 20-cm/8-inch pie plate or flan ring. Bake blind (see page 119) in a moderately hot oven (200 C, 400 F, Gas Mark 6) for 20 minutes, remove the paper and beans or cooking foil and bake for a further 10 minutes until golden. Remove from the oven and cool on a wire rack.

Blend a little of the milk with the cornflour and sugar in a bowl. Heat the remaining milk in a saucepan until hot and pour on to the blended mixture. Return to the saucepan and bring to the boil, stirring continuously. Cook for 3 minutes, take off the heat, stir in the egg yolk and cool. Dissolve the gelatine in the hot water and add to the cooled custard. Divide the custard in half and blend one half with the melted chocolate. Pour into the cooled flan case and leave to set.

Add the orange juice to the remaining custard. Whisk the egg white until stiff and fold into the orange custard. Pour on to the set chocolate layer and leave to set again. Serve the flan chilled, decorated with the whipped cream.

Golden treacle tart

— SERVES 4-6 —

1 recipe Shortcrust pastry (opposite page)
450 g/1 lb golden syrup
2 teaspoons finely grated lemon rind
25 g/1 oz butter
4 tablespoons single cream
2 eggs, beaten
whipped cream to decorate

Roll out the pastry on a lightly floured board or work surface to form a round large enough to line a 20-cm/8-inch flan ring. Place the flan ring on a greased baking tray and gently ease the pastry into the flan. Trim the edges of excess pastry and prick the base with a fork.

Gently heat the syrup in a saucepan with the lemon rind until hand-hot. Dice the butter into small pieces and stir into the syrup. Heat to dissolve, then leave until almost cold.

Beat the cream and eggs together and fold in the cool syrup mixture. Mix well, then pour into the prepared flan case. Bake in a moderate oven (180 C, 350 F, Gas Mark 4) for 40 minutes or until the pastry is crisp and the filling is set. Serve hot or cold, decorated with whipped cream.

Creamy custard tart

— SERVES 6 —

1 recipe Rich shortcrust pastry (opposite page)
3 large eggs, separated
25 g/1 oz castor sugar
300 ml/½ pint milk
few drops of vanilla essence
25 g/1 oz seedless raisins
ground nutmeg for sprinkling

Grease a 20-cm/8-inch flan tin. Roll out the pastry on a lightly floured board or work surface to a circle large enough to line the flan tin. Ease the pastry into the tin and trim away any excess dough.

Beat two egg whites and three egg yolks together in a bowl with the sugar, milk and vanilla. Strain through a fine nylon sieve. Brush the inside of the pastry case with the remaining egg white, lightly beaten. This forms a seal so that the custard does not soak into the tart while cooking. Sprinkle the base with the raisins and pour over the custard mixture. Sprinkle with ground nutmeg.

Bake in a moderately hot oven (200 C, 400 F, Gas Mark 6) for 15 minutes, then reduce the oven temperature to moderate (180 C, 350 F, Gas Mark 4) and bake for a further 15 minutes or until the pastry is cooked through and the custard is set. Serve hot or chilled.

Apple and pear dumplings

SERVES 4

2 dessert apples
2 dessert pears
1 recipe Shortcrust pastry (page 74)
4 tablespoons mixed dried fruit
1 tablespoon clear honey
2 tablespoons chopped mixed nuts
beaten egg or milk to glaze

Grease a baking tray. Peel and core the apples and pears, leaving the fruit whole.

Roll out the pastry on a lightly floured board or work surface and cut out two circles of dough slightly larger than the apples. Cut the remaining pastry into 2.5-cm/1-inch wide strips.

Mix the dried fruit, honey and nuts together in a bowl. Place each apple on a circle of dough and fill the centres with half of the fruit mixture. Carefully fold the pastry around the apples, securing the dough together by dampening the edges with a little water. Place seam-side down on the baking tray.

Fill the centres of the pears with the remaining fruit mixture. Dampen the pastry strips with water, then carefully wind around the pears to enclose them completely. Place upright on the baking tray. Use any pastry trimmings to make decorative leaves for the apples and pears. Glaze with beaten egg or milk and bake in a moderately hot oven (200 C, 400 F, Gas Mark 6) for 35-40 minutes or until golden. Serve with pouring custard or cream.

Pear frangipane tart

SERVES 4-6

1 recipe Rich shortcrust pastry (page 74)
3-4 firm dessert pears
350 g/4 oz sugar
300 ml/$\frac{1}{2}$ pint water
few drops of vanilla essence
FRANGIPANE
100 g/4 oz butter
100 g/4 oz castor sugar
2 eggs
100 g/4 oz ground almonds
25 g/1 oz flour
almond essence or Kirsch to taste
GLAZE
6 tablespoons apricot jam
2 tablespoons water

Roll out the pastry on a lightly floured board or work surface to a circle large enough to line a 20-cm/8-inch flan tin. Prick the bottom with a fork.

Meanwhile, peel, halve and core the pears. Boil the sugar in a saucepan with the water and vanilla. Add the pears and poach until tender, about 20-25 minutes. Remove with a slotted spoon and cool.

Prepare the frangipane by beating the butter with the sugar. Beat in the eggs, one at a time, then stir in the almonds and flour and flavour with almond essence or Kirsch to taste. Fill the flan with the frangipane and bake in a moderately hot oven (190 C, 375 F, Gas Mark 5) for about 25 minutes, or until cooked through, then cool.

Meanwhile, gently heat the apricot jam with the water and brush a little over the top of the tart. Place the poached pears on top and brush with the remaining glaze.

French apple tart

SERVES 6-8

PASTRY
100 g/4 oz butter or margarine
175 g/6 oz plain flour
2 teaspoons castor sugar
40 g/1½ oz ground almonds
1 egg yolk
1 tablespoon cold water
GLAZE
25 g/1 oz butter
50 g/2 oz castor sugar
FILLING
900 g/2 lb dessert apples, peeled, cored and
thickly sliced
apple slices to decorate

Prepare the pastry by rubbing the butter or margarine into the flour until the mixture resembles fine bread-crumbs. Stir in the sugar and almonds and mix well. Combine the egg yolk with the water and stir into the flour mixture. Mix to form a stiff dough. Chill for about 15 minutes.

Meanwhile, to make the glaze and filling, melt the butter in the base of a 23-cm/9-inch round, shallow, flameproof dish or cake tin. Add the sugar and cook over a gentle heat until the mixture turns golden. Remove from the heat. When the mixture has cooled slightly, layer the apples on top, packing the slices close together.

Roll out the pastry on a lightly floured board or work surface to form a round a little larger than the top of the cake tin or dish. Lift on to the apples and tuck the pastry in around the edges. Bake in a moderately hot oven (200 C, 400 F, Gas Mark 6) for 30-35 minutes. Turn out on to a serving dish, apple side uppermost, and decorate with apple slices. Serve hot or cold with cream.

Festive mince pies

MAKES 24

PASTRY
275 g/10 oz plain flour
25 g/1 oz ground almonds
175 g/6 oz butter or margarine
75 g/3 oz icing sugar
grated rind of 1 lemon
1 egg yolk
3 tablespoons milk
FILLING
225 g/8 oz mincemeat
1 tablespoon brandy
grated rind of 1 small orange
icing sugar to dust

Grease two tartlet tins. Mix the flour and ground almonds together in a bowl and rub in the butter or margarine until the mixture resembles fine breadcrumbs. Mix in the icing sugar and lemon rind. Combine the egg yolk with the milk and mix into the flour mixture. Form into a firm dough and chill for 30 minutes.

Roll out two-thirds of the pastry on a lightly floured board or work surface and, using a 7.5-cm/3-inch diameter pastry cutter, cut out 24 fluted circles. Carefully line the prepared tartlet moulds. Blend the mincemeat with the brandy and orange rind and spoon equal amounts into the pastry cases.

Gather the remaining dough and pastry trimmings and roll out again on a lightly floured board or work surface. Using a star-shaped pastry cutter, stamp out 24 stars to form the mince pie lids. Place on top of the fluted tartlets and bake in a moderately hot oven (200 C, 400 F, Gas Mark 6) for 20-25 minutes until light golden and cooked through.

Transfer to a wire rack and allow to cool. Serve warm, dusted with icing sugar.

Apricot bourdaloue tart

1 recipe Rich shortcrust pastry (page 74)
100 g/4 oz sugar
300 ml/½ pint water
675 g/1½ lb apricots, peeled, halved and stoned
2 egg yolks
50 g/2 oz castor sugar
grated rind of 1 orange
1½ tablespoons cornflour
1½ tablespoons plain flour
300 ml/½ pint milk
1 egg white
2 tablespoons toasted flaked almonds

Roll out the pastry on a lightly floured board or work surface to form a circle large enough to line a 20-cm/8-inch flan tin. Ease the pastry into the greased tin and trim away any excess. Prick the base with a fork, then bake 'blind' (see page 119) in a hot oven (220 C, 425 F, Gas Mark 7) for 15 minutes. Remove the cooking foil or paper and beans and bake for a further 10 minutes or until the pastry is cooked and golden. Cool the flan on a wire rack.

Meanwhile, dissolve the 100 g/4 oz sugar with the water in a saucepan and bring to the boil. Boil for 5 minutes, then add the apricots and simmer for 5 minutes, or until tender but still firm. Remove the apricots with a slotted spoon and set aside. Reduce the syrup until thick by boiling over a high heat for about 5 minutes.

Whisk the egg yolks and half the castor sugar together in a bowl until thick. Beat in the orange rind, cornflour and flour. Scald the milk in another saucepan and slowly pour the milk over the egg mixture, beating constantly. Return the mixture to the saucepan and cook for 3-5 minutes or until smooth and thick. Leave to cool. Whisk the egg white until frothy, then gradually whisk in the remaining sugar and beat until the mixture forms stiff peaks. Carefully fold the egg white mixture through the cooled orange mixture, using a metal spoon.

Spoon the orange filling into the cooked pastry case, creating a slight mound in the centre. Top with the apricot halves, cut side down. Brush or spoon over the cooled thick syrup and scatter with toasted almonds. Chill and serve.

Note: It is possible to substitute canned apricots for fresh ones. Use 1 (398-g/14-oz) can apricot halves and reduce the can syrup in a saucepan with 25 g/1 oz additional sugar for the syrup glaze.

Glazed strawberry flan

FLAN PASTRY
75 g/3 oz butter or margarine
175 g/6 oz plain flour
40 g/1½ oz castor sugar
2 egg yolks
3 teaspoons cold water
FILLING
25 g/1 oz butter or margarine
25 g/1 oz plain flour
300 ml/½ pint milk
25 g/1 oz castor sugar
1 egg yolk
1 tablespoon single cream
1 tablespoon sweet sherry (optional)
TOPPING
225 g/8 oz strawberries
4 tablespoons seedless strawberry or
raspberry jam
1 tablespoon lemon juice

Grease a 20-cm/8-inch flan tin. Prepare the flan pastry by rubbing the butter or margarine into the flour until the mixture resembles fine breadcrumbs. Stir in the sugar and mix well. Combine the egg yolks and water together and stir into the mixture. Form into a firm dough. Roll out on a lightly floured board or work surface to form a round large enough to line the base and sides of the tin. Trim away any excess pastry and bake 'blind' (see page 119) in a moderately hot oven (200 C, 400 F, Gas Mark 6) for 15-20 minutes. Remove the cooking foil or paper and beans and bake for a further 5-10 minutes or until cooked and golden. Cool on a wire rack.

Meanwhile, prepare the filling by melting the butter or margarine in a saucepan. Add the flour and cook, stirring, for 1 minute. Gradually add the milk and bring to the boil, stirring constantly, until slightly thickened. Allow to cool slightly then add the sugar, egg yolk, cream and sherry, if used. Pour into the base of the flan and allow to cool.

Hull the strawberries, except for four or five to be used for decoration, and arrange them, whole or halved, over the cooled filling. Prepare the glaze by heating the jam with the lemon juice in a saucepan, stirring until well mixed. Spoon over the strawberries and allow to cool and set. Chill the flan before serving with whipped cream.

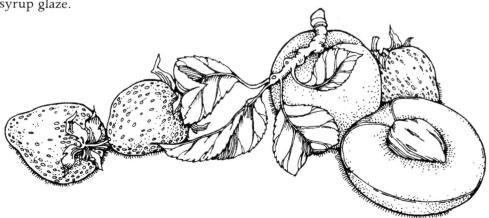

Apple strudel

SERVES 6

STRUDEL PASTRY
150 g/5 oz plain flour
pinch of salt
2 teaspoons oil
½ egg, beaten
about 100 ml/4 fl oz warm water
FILLING
450 g/1 lb cooking apples, peeled, cored
and sliced
50 g/2 oz currants
50 g/2 oz sultanas
1 teaspoon ground cinnamon
3 tablespoons breadcrumbs, toasted
25 g/1 oz butter, melted
icing sugar to dust

Grease a large baking tray. First prepare the strudel pastry by mixing the flour with the salt in a large bowl. Make a well in the centre and add the oil, egg and 2-3 tablespoons water. Start to mix, adding more warm water, to form a soft paste. Beat, using your hand, until smooth. Cover and leave for 15 minutes.

Meanwhile, mix the apples, currants, sultanas, cinnamon and 1 tablespoon of the breadcrumbs together.

Roll the pastry out on a well-floured board or work surface to about 1 cm/½ inch thickness. Lift on to a well-floured tea towel and leave for about 8 minutes. Carefully pull the pastry on all sides to stretch the dough. Stretch until very thin. Brush with a little of the melted butter and sprinkle with the remaining breadcrumbs. Scatter over the fruit and roll up.

Place on a baking tray in the shape of a horseshoe and brush with the remaining butter. Bake in a moderately hot oven (200 C, 400 F, Gas Mark 6) for 20-25 minutes until golden. Dust with the icing sugar and serve warm, cut in thick diagonal slices.

Strawberry mille feuilles

SERVES 4-6

1 (396-g/14-oz) packet frozen puff pastry,
thawed
4 tablespoons strawberry jam
1 tablespoon Kirsch or orange juice
300 ml/½ pint double cream
2 teaspoons castor sugar
350 g/12 oz strawberries, hulled and sliced
75 g/3 oz icing sugar
a few stalked strawberries to decorate

Roll out the pastry on a lightly floured board or work surface to form a 20 × 25-cm/8 × 10-inch rectangle. Cut lengthwise into three equal rectangles, and place on a dampened baking sheet. Bake in a hot oven (220 C, 425 F, Gas Mark 7) for 20 minutes until well risen and golden. Cool on a wire rack.

Using a sharp knife, trim the rectangles to the same size, crushing any trimmings to use later. Mix the jam with the Kirsch or orange juice and whip the cream with the castor sugar until it stands in soft peaks. Place one pastry strip on a serving plate. Top with half the jam and half the cream. Cover with half the sliced strawberries and the second pastry strip. Top with the remaining jam mixture and cream and cover with the remaining strawberries and the final pastry strip.

Mix the icing sugar with a little water to make a thick glacé icing. Spread over the top pastry strip and sprinkle a border of the crushed trimmings around the icing. Decorate with a few strawberries, halved but with their stalks on, and eat as soon as possible.

Strawberry palmiers

— MAKES 8 —

150 g/5 oz castor sugar
1 (397-g/14-oz) packet frozen puff pastry,
thawed
225 g/8 oz strawberries
450 ml/$\frac{3}{4}$ pint double cream
2 teaspoons icing sugar, sifted

Sprinkle a board or work surface with 25 g/1 oz of the sugar and roll out the pastry to a 30-cm/12-inch square. Using a sharp knife, trim the edges until completely square. Lightly brush with chilled water and sprinkle evenly with 50 g/2 oz of the remaining sugar. Fold two opposite sides together to meet in the centre. Press down lightly. Lightly brush the surface again with water and sprinkle evenly with the remaining sugar. Fold the same sides to the centre again and press down lightly. Finally fold up the two sides together and press down lightly to give a single roll that when cut across will form heart-shaped slices.

Cut the long folded roll across into 1-cm/$\frac{1}{2}$-inch slices, using a sharp knife. Place well apart on a dampened baking tray. Press each palmier to flatten slightly, then bake in a hot oven (220 C, 425 F, Gas Mark 7) for 10 minutes. Turn over carefully using a spatula and bake for a further 10 minutes. Remove from the oven and cool on a wire rack.

Reserve a few strawberries for decoration, then hull and halve the rest. Whip the cream until it forms soft peaks, then fold in the icing sugar. Place the cream in a piping bag fitted with a large star-shaped nozzle and pipe swirls of cream on to half of the palmiers. Top each palmier base with strawberries, then cover with another palmier. Decorate with the reserved strawberries, halved. Chill before serving.

Chocolate profiteroles

— SERVES 4-6 —

CHOUX PASTRY
50 g/2 oz butter
150 ml/$\frac{1}{4}$ pint water
pinch of salt
1 teaspoon castor sugar
100 g/4 oz plain flour
4 eggs, beaten
FILLING
300 ml/$\frac{1}{2}$ pint double cream
CHOCOLATE SAUCE
125 g/4$\frac{1}{2}$ oz plain chocolate
25 g/1 oz castor sugar
450 ml/$\frac{3}{4}$ pint water

Lightly grease a baking tray. Place the butter, water, salt, and sugar in a saucepan. Bring slowly to the boil, then immediately add the flour and stir quickly to form a paste, until the mixture leaves the sides of the saucepan clean. Allow the paste to cool slightly. When cool, beat in the eggs, a spoonful at a time. Place in a piping bag fitted with a large plain nozzle and pipe small rounds on to the prepared baking tray. Bake in a hot oven (220 C, 425 F, Gas Mark 7) for 15-20 minutes until crisp and dry. Remove from the oven and pierce each profiterole with a sharp knife to release any steam.

Whip the cream until it stands in soft peaks. Split each profiterole in half and fill with cream. Sandwich the halves back together again and place in a dish.

To make the sauce, melt the chocolate in a bowl over a saucepan of hot water. Boil the sugar and water together in another saucepan for about 5 minutes then add, spoon by spoon, to the chocolate. Simmer for a further 10 minutes until the chocolate sauce coats the back of a spoon. Spoon over the profiteroles.

Almond chocolate flan

SERVES 6

PASTRY
175 g/6 oz ground almonds
50 g/2 oz castor sugar
1 large egg white, lightly beaten
FILLING
300 ml/½ pint double cream
225 g/8 oz plain chocolate
whipped cream, chocolate curls and whole
hazelnuts to decorate

This rich chocolate flan is certainly worthy of the 24 hours chilling time required before eating. For best results, make it up to two or three days ahead.

First prepare the pastry by mixing the almonds with the castor sugar. Add the egg white and mix to a stiff dough. Chill for at least 1 hour, then roll out on a lightly floured board or work surface to form a circle large enough to line a 23-cm/9-inch fluted metal flan tin. Place the flan tin on a greased baking tray and carefully ease the pastry into the flan. The pastry is very fragile so it may be necessary to patch up any areas that become damaged while you line the flan tin. Bake in a moderate oven (180 c, 350 f, Gas Mark 4) for 35 minutes. Allow to cool in the tin.

Meanwhile, prepare the filling. Gently heat the cream in a saucepan. When warm, add the chocolate, broken into pieces, remove from the heat and stir until completely dissolved. Heat the chocolate and cream mixture further if the chocolate does not dissolve easily. Remove from the heat and beat until quite cold. Pour into the cold flan case and chill for at least 24 hours.

Serve the flan cut into wedges decorated with whipped cream, chocolate curls and whole hazelnuts.

Plum chiffon pie

SERVES 6

225 g/8 oz digestive biscuits
100 g/4 oz butter or margarine
450 g/1 lb plums, halved and stoned
3 tablespoons water
225 g/8 oz castor sugar
1 tablespoon powdered gelatine
3 egg whites
100 ml/4 fl oz double cream, whipped

Crush the biscuits in a blender or place in a plastic bag and crush with a rolling pin. Melt the butter in a saucepan, then stir in the crumbs and use to line the base and sides of a 23-cm/9-inch fluted flan tin.

Place the plums and water in a saucepan and cook gently until the fruit is soft. Purée in an electric blender or pass through a fine sieve. Combine 60 g/2½ oz of the sugar with the gelatine and half the plum purée in a saucepan. Bring to the boil then cool, stirring from time to time. Meanwhile, in another saucepan, boil the remaining plum purée with 60 g/2½ oz of the sugar and allow to cool.

Whisk the egg whites until they stand in firm peaks. Gradually whisk in the remaining sugar to form a stiff, glossy mixture. Fold in the plum and gelatine purée mixture and the whipped cream. Turn this mixture into the biscuit case, smoothing the surface. Dribble the sweetened plum purée over the top, then swirl with a knife to combine the two mixtures. Chill until set, about 2 hours.

Blackcurrant and ginger cheesecake

SERVES 6

100 g/4 oz butter
225 g/8 oz gingernut biscuits, crushed
450 g/1 lb full-fat cream cheese
50 g/2 oz castor sugar
6 tablespoons single cream
575 g/1¼ lb blackcurrants, topped and tailed
15 g/½ oz powdered gelatine
300 ml/½ pint double cream
1 egg white, stiffly whisked

Lightly grease a 23-cm/9-inch loose-bottomed cake tin with a little of the butter. Melt the remainder in a small saucepan. When melted, add the gingernut crumbs and mix well to coat evenly. Use to line the base of the tin and chill until set.

In a mixing bowl, beat the cream cheese and sugar together until smooth and creamy. Stir in the single cream and 450 g/1 lb of the blackcurrants. Dissolve the gelatine in 2 tablespoons of boiling water and stir into the blackcurrant mixture. Spoon this mixture over the chilled cheesecake crust. Chill until set, about 1 hour.

Meanwhile, whip the double cream until it stands in soft peaks, then fold in the whisked egg white. Using a spoon, swirl this cream mixture over the top of the chilled cheesecake. Use the remaining blackcurrants to sprinkle over the cream and decorate the edge of the cheesecake. Chill for about 15 minutes before serving.

Creamy New York cheesecake

SERVES 8-10

BASE
175 g/6 oz digestive biscuits
75 g/3 oz butter, melted
FILLING
450 g/1 lb full-fat cream cheese
450 g/1 lb cottage cheese, sieved
275 g/10 oz castor sugar
2 teaspoons vanilla essence
pinch of salt
5 eggs, separated
1 (100-ml/4-fl oz) can evaporated milk
100 ml/4 fl oz double cream
3 tablespoons plain flour
1 tablespoon lemon juice

Heat the oven to hot (230 c, 450 f, Gas Mark 8). Lightly grease the base and sides of a 23-cm/9-inch loose-bottomed spring-release cake tin. Crush the biscuits in a plastic bag with a rolling pin or in an electric blender. Mix the crumbs with the butter, then press on to the base of the tin. Chill for 15-20 minutes or until the base has set.

Meanwhile, in a large bowl mix the cream cheese, cottage cheese, sugar, vanilla, salt and egg yolks together, beating until smooth and creamy. Add the evaporated milk, cream and flour. Whisk the egg whites until they stand in stiff peaks and fold into the cheese mixture with the lemon juice. Turn this mixture into the tin and place in the oven. Immediately reduce the oven temperature to moderate (180 c, 350 f, Gas Mark 4). Bake for 45 minutes, then turn off the oven. Allow the cheesecake to cool in the oven with the door slightly ajar. Chill before serving.

Proper puddings

. . . like mother used to make — both baked and steamed

In the height of the summer or the depth of the winter, it is rare to find anyone who can bypass that traditional British treat, the baked or steamed pudding. It is a fact that on these puddings the British stake their culinary reputation. And rightly so, for British puddings like Traditional plum duff with custard sauce, Bread and butter pudding, Apple charlotte and Sussex pond pudding have long and honourable pedigrees.

To do justice to this heritage and to ensure that it continues, I have developed some less grand, less time-consuming but just as delicious variations such as crumbles and cobblers. The only threat to the steamed, baked or boiled pudding's existence is the modern trend toward slim bodies and therefore meagre or at least restrained appetites. Such being the case, reconciliation lies in a weekend pudding treat rather than an everyday feast.

This section, however, is not just a collection of British favourites, for continental specialities such as Fruit savarin, Alpine chocolate pudding and Clafoutis have also been included. Enjoy them in the same spirit as the British favourites and you'll soon forget any real or imaginary food boundaries.

Honey and lemon surprise pudding and Traditional plum duff (overleaf); Greengage cobbler (page 88)

Honey and lemon surprise pudding

225 g/8 oz self-raising flour
pinch of salt
100 g/4 oz shredded suet
100 g/4 oz fresh breadcrumbs
50 g/2 oz soft brown sugar
350 g/12 oz clear honey
1 lemon
whipped cream to serve

Grease a 1-litre/2-pint pudding basin. Sift the flour and salt into a bowl and stir in the suet. Add sufficient cold water to make a soft dough, then knead on a lightly floured surface until smooth. Roll out the dough to form a circle about 25 cm/10 inches in diameter. Cut a right-angled segment out of the circle and set aside. Moisten the cut edges of the dough circle with water, press and seal them together and then lift the dough and ease it into the pudding basin. Press the dough gently against the sides and base of the basin, trimming away any excess.

Mix the breadcrumbs and sugar together and place half in the pudding. Pour over half the honey. Clean the lemon and prick several times with a fork. Position it carefully, upright, in the centre of the pudding. Spoon the remaining breadcrumb mixture around and over the lemon and pour over the remaining honey.

Lightly knead the remaining dough segment and trimmings and roll out to form a circle large enough to cover the basin. Dampen the pastry rim with water and carefully place the dough lid on the pudding, trimming away any excess dough. Press the edges together firmly to seal the pudding. Cover with greased greaseproof paper and a piece of greased cooking foil pleated to allow for expansion (see page 118) and secure with string.

Place in a steamer or stand it on a trivet in a saucepan half full of water and steam over a moderate heat for 3¾ hours. To serve, turn out the pudding on to a serving dish and cut open, piercing the lemon to let out any juices. Make sure you give a piece of lemon with each serving, since this is an essential part of the pudding. Serve immediately with whipped cream.

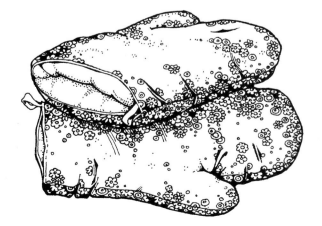

Traditional plum duff with custard sauce

PUDDING
50 g/2 oz currants
50 g/2 oz raisins
50 g/2 oz sultanas
2 tablespoons sweet sherry
2 tablespoons orange juice
100 g/4 oz self-raising flour, sifted
1 teaspoon ground cinnamon
1 teaspoon ground mixed spice
100 g/4 oz fresh white breadcrumbs
100 g/4 oz shredded suet
75 g/3 oz light soft brown sugar
1 egg, beaten
4 tablespoons milk
CUSTARD SAUCE
2 egg yolks
15 g/½ oz sugar
2 drops vanilla essence
300 ml/¼ pint milk

Grease a 1-litre/2-pint pudding basin. Put the currants, raisins and sultanas in a bowl. Pour over the sherry and orange juice and leave, covered, for 2-4 hours to enable the fruit to marinate and swell in size.

Mix the flour with the cinnamon and mixed spice. Add the breadcrumbs, suet and sugar, mixing well. Add the fruit with the juice, the egg and milk. Mix well with a wooden spoon until blended. Turn into the prepared pudding basin. Cover with greased greaseproof paper and a piece of greased cooking foil pleated to allow for expansion (see page 118). Secure with string. Place in a steamer or on a trivet in a saucepan half full of water and steam over a moderate heat for 1¾-2 hours.

Meanwhile, prepare the custard sauce. In a basin, beat the egg yolks. Heat the sugar, vanilla essence and milk in a saucepan until hot but not boiling. Whisk into the egg yolks. Place the basin over a saucepan of hot water, but do not allow the water to boil or the eggs will curdle. Cook, stirring continuously, until the custard coats the back of the spoon, about 20-25 minutes.

To serve, turn out the pudding on to a warmed serving dish. Serve with the hot custard sauce.

Christmas pudding

SERVES 6-8

150 g/5 oz fresh wholewheat breadcrumbs
100 g/4 oz plain flour
100 g/4 oz sultanas
100 g/4 oz raisins
150 g/5 oz currants
100 g/4 oz shredded suet
60 g/2½ oz chopped mixed peel
60 g/2½ oz glacé cherries
100 g/4 oz Demerara sugar
1 small cooking apple, peeled, cored and grated
1 carrot, peeled and grated
40 g/1½ oz blanched almonds, chopped
pinch of ground nutmeg
1 teaspoon black treacle
2 large eggs, beaten
200 ml/7 fl oz brown ale
50 ml/2 fl oz brandy

Grease a 1-litre/2-pint pudding basin. Mix all the ingredients together in a large mixing bowl, using a wooden spoon. Place the mixture in the prepared basin, smoothing down and levelling off the top. Cover with greased greaseproof paper and a piece of greased cooking foil pleated to allow for expansion (see page 118). Secure with string. Place in a steamer or on a trivet in a saucepan half full of water. Steam steadily for 6 hours. When cooked, store in a cool, damp-free place.

To serve, steam as above for a further 3 hours, then turn out on to a serving plate. Flame with extra brandy and accompany with cream, custard or brandy butter.

Sussex pond pudding

SERVES 4

225 g/8 oz self-raising flour
1 teaspoon salt
75 g/3 oz shredded suet
50 g/2 oz castor sugar
50 g/2 oz currants
about 150 ml/¼ pint water
FILLING
225 g/8 oz butter
50 g/2 oz mixed dried fruit
50 g/2 oz chopped mixed peel
100 g/4 oz glacé cherries
2 tablespoons mincemeat
1 eating apple, peeled, cored and
coarsely grated

Mix the flour, salt, suet, sugar and currants together. Add the water and mix to a soft dough. Knead on a lightly floured work surface until smooth. Divide in half and roll out each piece to a 15-cm/6-inch circle.

To make the filling, cream the butter and add the dried fruit, peel, cherries, mincemeat and apple. Chill lightly then form into a ball. Place the mixture in the centre of one round, dampen the edges, cover with the second circle of dough and pinch the two edges together. Enclose in a piece of greased cooking foil and secure with string. Steam in a steamer or on a trivet in a saucepan half full of water for 2½-3 hours. Remove the cooking foil and serve on a warmed dish.

Apple charlotte

10 slices white bread
60 g/2½ oz butter
¼ teaspoon ground cinnamon
50 g/2 oz dark soft brown sugar
575 g/1¼ lb cooking apples, peeled, cored and
thinly sliced
juice of 1 lemon

Trim the crusts from the bread and reserve. Lightly butter the trimmed bread slices with 40 g/1½ oz of the butter. Line a 900-ml/1½-pint pudding basin with the bread slices, buttered side inwards, reserving a few bread slices for the lid.

Using an electric blender, reduce the reserved crusts to 50 g/2 oz of crumbs. Melt the remaining butter in a small saucepan. Add the crumbs and cook until golden. Stir in the cinnamon and sugar. Allow to cool.

Toss the apples in the lemon juice to prevent discoloration, then layer in the basin with the breadcrumbs. Cover with the reserved bread slices, buttered side up. Cover with cooking foil and secure with string. Bake in a moderately hot oven (200 C, 400 F, Gas Mark 6) for about 1¼ hours. Allow to cool a little before turning out on to a warmed serving dish or serve straight from the basin. Serve with cream or custard.

Cherry or plum cobbler

450 g/1 lb cherries or plums, stoned
50 g/2 oz castor sugar
grated rind and juice of 1 orange
COBBLER TOPPING
100 g/4 oz butter or margarine
225 g/8 oz self-raising flour
25 g/1 oz castor sugar
about 150 ml/¼ pint milk
beaten egg or milk to glaze
25 g/1 oz Demerara sugar

Place the cherries or plums in a saucepan with the sugar, orange rind, orange juice and about 2 tablespoons water. Bring to the boil and simmer for 2-3 minutes. Place in a 900-ml/1½-pint pie dish.

Make the topping by rubbing the butter or margarine into the flour until the mixture resembles fine breadcrumbs. Stir in the sugar and milk and mix to a soft dough. Knead gently, then roll out on a lightly floured surface to about 1.5 cm/½ inch thickness. Cut out circles of dough using a 4-cm/1½-inch diameter biscuit cutter. Arrange in an overlapping pattern around the top of the fruit.

Glaze the topping with beaten egg or milk and sprinkle with the Demerara sugar. Bake in a hot oven (230 C, 450 F, Gas Mark 8) for 15 minutes until well risen and golden. Serve with single cream or custard.

Greengages can also be used as a variation.

Cherry upside-down pudding

SERVES 6

TOPPING
25 g/1 oz butter
50 g/2 oz soft brown sugar
75 g/3 oz glacé cherries, halved
75 g/3 oz walnuts
SPONGE BASE
100 g/4 oz butter
100 g/4 oz castor sugar
2 eggs, beaten
2 tablespoons coffee essence
175 g/6 oz self-raising flour

Lightly grease a 15-cm/6-inch round cake tin. Prepare the topping by melting the butter in a saucepan. Add the sugar, cherries and walnuts. Spread over the base of the tin.

Prepare the sponge base by creaming the butter with the sugar, until soft and creamy. Beat in the eggs, a little at a time, with the coffee essence. Using a metal spoon, fold in the flour. Spoon the sponge mixture over the cherry and walnut base and bake in a moderate oven (180 C, 350 F, Gas Mark 4) for 50-55 minutes or until the sponge has cooked and shrunk away slightly from the sides of the tin.

To serve, turn out the pudding on to a warmed serving dish. Serve hot with whipped or clotted cream.

Bread and butter pudding

SERVES 4-6

40 g/1½ oz butter, softened
8 large slices bread, crusts removed
50 g/2 oz currants
50 g/2 oz sultanas
600 ml/1 pint milk
50 g/2 oz castor sugar
2 eggs
2-3 drops vanilla essence
ground nutmeg to sprinkle
2 tablespoons Demerara sugar

Butter each slice of bread on both sides and cut into four triangles. Place a layer of bread in the bottom of a 1.5-litre/2½-pint ovenproof dish. Sprinkle with half the currants and sultanas. Top with the remaining bread triangles and dried fruit.

Heat the milk with the sugar in a saucepan until dissolved. Beat the eggs with the vanilla essence in a small bowl. Pour the milk on to the egg mixture and whisk until well mixed. Strain through a fine sieve over the bread and fruit mixture and leave to soak for 10-15 minutes. Sprinkle with ground nutmeg, then bake in a moderate oven (180 C, 350 F, Gas Mark 4) for 1¼ hours until just golden and set. Sprinkle with the Demerara sugar to serve.

Alpine chocolate pudding

SERVES 6

1 teaspoon butter
175 g/6 oz plain chocolate
300 ml/½ pint milk
8 slices fresh white bread, crusts removed
and cubed
175 g/6 oz butter, softened
175 g/6 oz castor sugar
6 eggs, separated
50 g/2 oz ground almonds
grated rind of ½ orange
2 tablespoons crushed macaroons
custard sauce (see page 86) to serve

Grease a 1-litre/2-pint pudding basin with the butter. In a small saucepan, melt the chocolate in a little of the milk over a low heat. Soak the bread in the remaining milk for 5 minutes.

Cream the butter and sugar together until soft and creamy. Beat in the egg yolks, one at a time, then mix in the melted chocolate. Combine the soaked bread and milk with the chocolate mixture to form a smooth mixture. Finally beat in the ground almonds. Whisk the egg whites until stiff and fold into the mixture. Mix the orange rind and macaroons together and sprinkle the mixture over the bottom of the pudding basin. Pour the chocolate mixture into the prepared basin. Cover with greased greaseproof paper and a piece of greased cooking foil pleated to allow for expansion (see page 118). Secure with string.

Place in a steamer or on a trivet in a saucepan half full of water and steam steadily for 1 hour. Turn out and serve hot with custard sauce.

Constantine grape pudding

SERVES 4

50 g/2 oz rice flour
75 g/3 oz castor sugar
75 g/3 oz butter
3 eggs, separated
50 g/2 oz self-raising flour
25 g/1 oz plain cake crumbs
almond essence to taste
1-2 tablespoons milk
SAUCE
4 sugar cubes
2 tablespoons greengage jam
225 ml/8 fl oz water
1 teaspoon arrowroot
100 g/4 oz green seedless grapes

Grease a 1-litre/1½-pint pudding basin. Coat the inside of the basin with a little of the rice flour and sugar.

Cream the butter with the remaining castor sugar and beat in the egg yolks. Fold in the flour, the remaining rice flour, cake crumbs, almond essence to taste and milk to give a stiff batter. Whisk the egg whites until they stand in firm peaks. Fold into the batter. Spoon into the prepared basin and cover with greased greaseproof paper and a piece of cooking foil pleated to allow for expansion (see page 118). Secure with string. Steam in a steamer or on a trivet in a saucepan half full of water for 1½ hours.

Meanwhile, prepare the sauce. Place the sugar cubes, jam and water in a saucepan. Heat to dissolve. Blend the arrowroot with a little water and stir into the jam mixture. Bring to the boil, stirring, and allow to thicken. Stir in the grapes.

To serve, turn out the pudding on to a warmed serving dish and pour over the hot grape sauce.

St Clement's syrup sponge pudding

SERVES 4-6

4 tablespoons golden syrup
2 medium oranges
100 g/4 oz butter or margarine
100 g/4 oz castor sugar
2 eggs, beaten
grated rind and juice of 1 small orange and
1 small lemon
125 g/4 oz self-raising flour, sifted
warm golden syrup to serve

Grease a 1-litre/2-pint pudding basin. Spoon the golden syrup into the base. Using a sharp knife, slice the unpeeled oranges very thinly into rounds and press on to the base and sides of the basin. Cream the butter or margarine and sugar until soft and fluffy. Gradually beat in the eggs, orange rind and juice and lemon rind and juice. Using a metal spoon, fold in the flour. Spoon this mixture into the prepared basin.

Cover the pudding with greased greaseproof paper and a piece of greased cooking foil pleated to allow for expansion (see page 118). Secure with string. Place in a steamer or on a trivet in a saucepan half full of water and steam over a moderate heat for 1½-1¾ hours. To serve, turn out the pudding on to a warmed serving dish and serve with warm golden syrup.

Jam or treacle sponge pudding

SERVES 4-6

100 g/4 oz butter or margarine
100 g/4 oz castor sugar
grated rind of 1 lemon
2 eggs, beaten
175 g/6 oz self-raising flour
pinch of salt
2 tablespoons golden syrup or jam

Grease a 1-litre/2-pint pudding basin or about 4-6 small dariole moulds.

Cream the butter or margarine with the sugar and lemon rind in a bowl until light and fluffy. Add the eggs and beat well. Sift the flour and salt together and fold into the creamed mixture. Spoon the jam or syrup into the bottom of the pudding basin or dariole moulds and pour the sponge mixture on top. Cover with greased greaseproof paper and a piece of greased cooking foil pleated to allow for expansion (see page 118). Secure with string.

Steam in a steamer or on a trivet in a saucepan half full of water. Allow 1½-2 hours for the large pudding and 40-45 minutes for the smaller moulds. Turn out and serve with custard.

Variations

Dried fruit or coconut sponge pudding: Prepare the recipe as above but add 50 g/2 oz dried fruit or desiccated coconut to the sponge mixture. Omit the golden syrup or jam.

Chocolate sponge pudding: Prepare the recipe as above but add 25 g/1 oz cocoa powder and 25 g/1 oz chocolate polka dots (optional) to the sponge mixture. Omit the golden syrup or jam.

91

Clafoutis

450 g/1 lb red cherries, stoned
100 g/4 oz castor sugar
150 g/5 oz plain flour
2 eggs, beaten
300 ml/½ pint milk
1 tablespoon cherry brandy (optional)

Place the cherries in the base of a lightly greased 1-litre/2-pint shallow ovenproof dish. Sprinkle with 25 g/1 oz of the sugar.

Place the flour in a bowl, make a well in the centre and add the eggs and milk. Gradually work the flour into the eggs and milk and beat to make a smooth batter. Stir in the remaining sugar and cherry brandy, if used. Pour over the cherries and bake in a moderately hot oven (190 C, 375 F, Gas Mark 5) for about 55 minutes or until well risen and firm to the touch. Serve warm with cream.

Variation

Plum clafoutis: Prepare as above but use 450 g/1 lb small firm red or yellow plums instead of the cherries. Stone the plums but keep whole before using. Use 1 tablespoon sweet sherry instead of the cherry brandy.

Cider baked apples

4 large cooking or dessert apples, cored
100 g/4 oz dried apricots, chopped and
macerated overnight in 2 tablespoons brandy or
orange juice
4 teaspoons soft brown sugar
1 tablespoon currants
8 tablespoons dry cider

Make a shallow cut around the circumference of each apple to prevent the skins from bursting during cooking. Mix the apricots and their juice with the brown sugar and currants and use to stuff the centres of the apples. Place in an ovenproof dish. Spoon over the cider, cover and bake in a moderate oven (180 C, 350 F, Gas Mark 4) for about 45 minutes, basting from time to time, until the apples are tender.

Serve the apples hot, basted with the cider syrup and accompanied with cream.

Variation

Cider baked pears: Prepare as above but use 4 large firm cooking pears instead of the apples. Core and make a shallow cut around their circumferences before stuffing.

Oat and apple crumble

450 g/1 lb cooking apples, peeled, cored and
thinly sliced
100 g/4 oz soft brown sugar
6 cloves
40 g/1½ oz butter or margarine
100 g/4 oz rolled oats
apple slices to decorate (optional)

Mix the apple with 50 g/2 oz of the sugar and place in a
900-ml/1½-pint ovenproof dish. Scatter the cloves over
the apple. Melt the butter in a saucepan and add the
remaining sugar. Cook until the sugar dissolves. Remove
from the heat and add the oats. Turn the oats over in the
butter mixture to coat. Spoon over the apple mixture and
bake in a moderately hot oven (190 C, 375 F, Gas Mark 5)
for 30-40 minutes. Decorate with dessert apple slices, if
liked, and serve with custard or cream.

Variation

Oat, apple and blackberry crumble: Prepare as above
but use 225 g/8 oz hulled blackberries with 225 g/8 oz
peeled, cored and sliced apples.

Plum gingerbread pudding

675 g/1½ lb plums, halved and stoned
175 g/6 oz light muscovado sugar
50 g/2 oz unsalted butter
50 g/2 oz molasses sugar
50 g/2 oz pure cane sugar
5 tablespoons milk
2 eggs, beaten
225 g/8 oz plain flour
1 teaspoon ground mixed spice
1 teaspoon ground cinnamon
2 teaspoons ground ginger
½ teaspoon bicarbonate of soda

Mix the plums with the muscovado sugar and place in a
1-litre/1¾-pint greased ovenproof dish. In a saucepan,
heat the butter with the molasses sugar and cane sugar
until bubbling. Add the milk and leave to cool for 10
minutes. Add the eggs and mix well to blend.

Sift the flour with the spices and bicarbonate of soda
and beat into the syrup mixture. Pour over the plums,
spreading evenly. Bake in a moderate oven (180 C, 350 F,
Gas Mark 4) for 45 minutes. Serve hot with custard.

Fruit savarin

SAVARIN
1 teaspoon castor sugar
175 ml/6 fl oz milk
15 g/½ oz dried yeast
225 g/8 oz plain flour, sifted
pinch of salt
3 eggs, beaten
100 g/4 oz butter, melted
GLAZE
150 g/5 oz granulated sugar
225 ml/8 fl oz water
juice of ½ lemon
5 tablespoons dark rum
FILLING
450 g/1 lb mixed fresh fruit salad (for example,
oranges, grapes, cherries and pears)
whipped cream to decorate

Grease a 23-cm/9-inch plain ring mould. In a saucepan, mix the sugar with the milk and heat until lukewarm. Sprinkle the yeast over the milk and leave until frothy, about 10-15 minutes.

Mix the flour and salt in a large bowl. Combine the risen yeast liquid with the eggs and melted butter. Gradually mix into the flour, stirring and beating well to produce a smooth batter. Turn into the prepared mould and cover with oiled cling film. Leave in a warm place until the mixture has risen to the top of the tin.

Bake the savarin in a moderately hot oven (200 c, 400 f, Gas Mark 6) for 40 minutes or until golden and cooked through. Turn out of the tin and cool on a wire rack.

To prepare the glaze, mix the sugar with the water in a saucepan. Bring to the boil and boil steadily for 5 minutes or until the glaze has reduced by about half. Add the lemon juice and rum and mix well. Prick the cooked savarin all over with a fine skewer and transfer to a serving dish. Spoon the warm glaze over the savarin and leave to soak in.

Allow the savarin to cool completely then chill for 1 hour. Serve the savarin filled with fresh fruit salad and decorated with swirls of whipped cream.

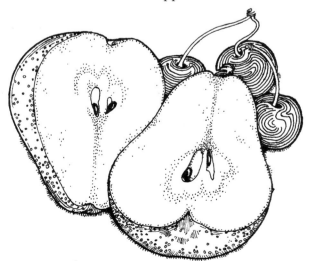

Treacle roll

275 g/10 oz self-raising flour
150 g/5 oz shredded suet
75 g/3 oz Demerara sugar
1 egg, beaten
about 150 ml/¼ pint milk
50 g/2 oz fresh white breadcrumbs
225 g/8 oz golden syrup
50 g/2 oz hazelnuts, chopped
custard sauce (page 86)

Mix the flour, suet and 50 g/2 oz of the sugar together. Mix the egg and milk together and add to the suet mixture. Mix to a firm dough. Roll out on a lightly floured surface to a 40 × 30-cm/15 × 12-inch rectangle.

Sprinkle the breadcrumbs over the dough to within 1.5 cm/½ inch of the edge. Spoon over the golden syrup and half the hazelnuts. Fold the edges of the dough just over the filling, to prevent it oozing out. Dampen the edges and roll up the dough from the short edge like a Swiss roll, sealing well.

Place seam side down in a well-greased 27.5 × 10-cm/ 11 × 4-inch loaf tin. Mix the remaining nuts and sugar together and scatter over the top of the roll.

Bake in a moderate oven (180 c, 350 f, Gas Mark 4) for about 1¼ hours, covering with a piece of cooking foil if it becomes too brown during the cooking time.

Serve the treacle roll cut into thick slices with the custard sauce.

Spicy orange bake

1 (450-g/1-lb) packet white bread mix
50 g/2 oz Demerara sugar
1 teaspoon ground cinnamon
1 egg, beaten
GLAZE
100 ml/4 fl oz concentrated frozen orange juice,
thawed
2 teaspoons clear honey

Make up the bread mix according to the manufacturer's instructions and divide into about 16 pieces. Roll each into a small ball.

Mix the sugar and cinnamon together on a plate. Dip the dough balls in the beaten egg and then roll in the sugar and spice mixture. Place on a greased baking tray in a pyramid shape. Cover loosely with oiled cling film and leave until the dough has doubled in size.

Bake in a preheated hot oven (220 c, 425 f, Gas Mark 7) for 35-40 minutes, or until the bread is well risen and brown.

Meanwhile, mix the orange juice with the honey in a small saucepan and cook until reduced to half. Pour the orange glaze over the hot baked bread and leave to soak in. Serve warm or cold, cut into wedges.

Frozen assets

. . . deliciously cool recipes for iced desserts

There are few sounds more enticing to children (and adults too) than that of the ice cream man. It conjures up wonderful ideas of smooth-as-silk ice cream with fruity toppings – old favourites, new flavours and fantastic creations. Sadly, shop-bought or street-bought varieties seldom live up to those expectations, so it is well worth the effort to make your own ice cream, sorbet or water ice at home.

Experiment with flavours and try combining them – after all, isn't that how raspberry ripple and Neapolitan were created?

Choose complementary sauces and toppings: rich chocolate or fudge, for instance, for the plainer ices and more subtle fruity ones for the rich combination types.

For best results, take the ice cream from the freezer about 30-60 minutes before serving and keep it in the refrigerator to allow it to soften slightly. Good old-fashioned ice cream made with milk, eggs and cream will not scoop as easily as the soft-scoop bought variety.

But don't just serve ice cream scooped into a glass or on a cone. To make it especially delicious, use it to fill a meringue nest or gâteau, or to top a seasonal fruit dessert.

Back left, clockwise: *Pineapple, Blackcurrant, Orange, Melon and champagne and Lemon sorbets;* Back right, clockwise: *Rich vanilla, Rich ginger, Rich chocolate ice creams;* Foreground, left to right: *Rich pistachio and Rich strawberry ice creams (recipes overleaf)*

Lemon water ice or sorbet

WATER ICE
750 ml/1¼ pints water
thinly pared rind and juice of 3 large lemons
200 g/7 oz sugar cubes
1 egg white
SORBET
1 egg white

To make the lemon water ice, place the water, lemon rind and sugar in a saucepan. Bring slowly to the boil to dissolve the sugar, then simmer for 5 minutes. Allow to cool, then remove the lemon rind and add the lemon juice. Pour into freezer trays and freeze until half frozen.

Whisk the egg white until it stands in firm peaks. Whisk the half-frozen mixture then fold in the egg white. Return to the freezer trays or to a 900-ml/1½-pint mould and freeze until firm. Serve in scoops or turn out and serve with crisp dessert biscuits.

To make a sorbet, prepare the water ice mixture as above. Whisk an additional egg white until it stands in stiff peaks and fold with the first egg white into the half-frozen mixture. Return to the freezer trays and freeze until firm. This mixture has a softer consistency and so cannot be moulded. Lemon water ice or sorbet may be scooped into frozen hollowed-out fruit cases just before serving or the fruit cases may be filled with the half-frozen mixture and frozen until firm.

Variations

Orange water ice or sorbet: Follow the recipe for Lemon water ice or sorbet but use the thinly pared rind and juice of 1 lemon with the thinly pared rind and juice of 3 oranges instead of lemons.
Raspberry, strawberry or pineapple water ice or sorbet: Follow the recipe for Lemon water ice or sorbet but use 300 ml/½ pint sieved raspberry or strawberry purée or 300 ml/½ pint puréed pineapple pulp with the thinly pared rind and juice of 3 lemons. Reduce the water in the recipe to 450 ml/¾ pint.
Blackberry or blackcurrant water ice or sorbet: Follow the recipe for Lemon water ice or sorbet but use 300 ml/½ pint sieved blackberry or blackcurrant purée with the thinly pared rind and juice of ½ lemon instead of the thinly pared rind and juice of 3 lemons. Reduce the water in the recipe to 450 ml/¾ pint. If available, add 5-6 sweet-scented geranium leaves to the water and remove with the lemon rind.
Melon and Champagne water ice or sorbet: Follow the recipe for Lemon water ice or sorbet but use 300 ml/½ pint melon purée (made with about 2 medium Cantaloupe melons or half a small water melon) with the finely pared rind and juice of ½ lemon instead of the finely pared rind and juice of 3 lemons. Reduce the water content to 450 ml/¾ pint and add 450 ml/¾ pint chilled Champagne to the cool mixture before freezing.
Madeira water ice or sorbet: Follow the recipe for Lemon water ice or sorbet but use 450 ml/¾ pint Madeira instead of 750 ml/1¼ pints of the water.

Rich vanilla ice cream

300 ml/½ pint single cream
3 eggs, beaten
40 g/1½ oz castor sugar
2 teaspoons vanilla essence
150 ml/¼ pint double cream

Place the single cream, eggs and sugar in a double boiler or in a bowl over a saucepan of simmering water and cook, stirring constantly, until the mixture coats the back of a spoon. Remove from the heat, stir in the vanilla essence and cool. Pour this custard base into freezer trays and freeze until half frozen.

Meanwhile, whip the double cream until it just forms soft peaks. Whisk the half-frozen custard until smooth then fold in the whipped cream. Return to the freezer trays and freeze until firm. Serve with fruit, crisp dessert biscuits or wafers.

Variations

Rich chocolate ice cream: Follow the recipe for Rich vanilla ice cream but use 75 g/3 oz melted chocolate instead of the vanilla essence.
Rich ginger ice cream: Follow the recipe for Rich vanilla ice cream but use 50 g/2 oz chopped preserved ginger and 2 tablespoons ginger wine instead of the vanilla essence.
Rich pistachio ice cream: Follow the recipe for Rich vanilla ice cream but use 50 g/2 oz finely chopped pistachio nuts instead of the vanilla essence. Fold the nuts into the mixture with the whipped cream. Tint the ice cream pale green with food colouring, if liked.
Rich raspberry or strawberry ice cream: Follow the recipe for Rich vanilla ice cream but use 250 ml/8 fl oz sieved raspberry or strawberry purée (made with about 225 g/8 oz fresh raspberries or strawberries) instead of the vanilla essence.
Rich coffee ice cream: Follow the recipe for Rich vanilla ice cream but use 4 teaspoons instant coffee granules, dissolved in 2 teaspoons boiling water, instead of the vanilla essence.
Rich banana or peach ice cream: Follow the recipe for Rich vanilla ice cream but use 3 small mashed or puréed bananas or 3 puréed peaches, peeled and stoned, instead of the vanilla essence.
Rich praline ice cream: Follow the recipe for Rich vanilla ice cream but use 75 g/3 oz crushed praline or nut brittle instead of the vanilla essence. Fold into the mixture with the whipped cream.

Coconut peach sundae

SERVES 4

COCONUT CHIP ICE CREAM
600 ml/1 pint double cream
100 g/4 oz desiccated coconut
50 g/2 oz icing sugar, sifted
1 egg, separated
100 g/4 oz plain chocolate, grated or
100 g/4 oz chocolate polka dots
SUNDAE
4 fresh peaches or 8 canned peach halves
1 recipe Melba sauce (page 48)
whipped cream and toasted coconut flakes
to decorate

Place the cream and coconut in a saucepan and cook, over a low heat, for about 10 minutes. Stir in the sugar and allow to cool. When cool, beat in the egg yolk and pour into freezer trays. Freeze until half frozen. Whisk the half-frozen ice cream until smooth then fold in the chocolate. Whisk the egg white until stiff and fold into the ice cream. Return to the freezer trays and freeze until firm.

Meanwhile, if using fresh peaches, poach them in boiling water with a little sugar until tender, about 4 minutes. Cool, peel away the skin, halve and stone.

To assemble the sundaes, place a scoop of coconut ice cream in the base of four individual containers. Top each with two peach halves and Melba sauce. Decorate with whipped cream and toasted coconut flakes. Serve with crisp dessert biscuits.

Banana splits with hot fudge sauce

SERVES 4

FUDGE SAUCE
25 g/1 oz plain chocolate
15 g/½ oz butter
2 tablespoons warm milk
100 g/4 oz soft brown sugar
3 teaspoons golden syrup
2-3 drops vanilla essence
BANANA SPLITS
4 large ripe bananas, peeled
1 recipe Rich vanilla ice cream (opposite page)
150 ml/¼ pint double cream
25 g/1 oz walnuts, finely chopped
fresh cherries to decorate (optional)

First prepare the sauce by melting the chocolate in a bowl over a saucepan of simmering water. Add the butter and stir until smooth and glossy. Gradually blend in the milk. Place this mixture with the sugar and golden syrup in a saucepan and heat gently to dissolve the sugar. Bring to the boil and cook for 5 minutes. Add the vanilla essence and keep warm.

Meanwhile, split each banana in half and quickly sandwich together with the ice cream in four individual dishes. Whip the cream until it stands in soft peaks. Spoon or pipe decoratively over the bananas and ice cream. Sprinkle with the nuts and decorate with the cherries, if used. Serve with the hot fudge sauce.

Frozen hazelnut and banana yogurt

———— SERVES 4 ————

4 medium bananas
grated rind and juice of 1 lemon
1-2 tablespoons dark rum
300 ml/½ pint natural yogurt
2 tablespoons soft brown sugar
2 egg whites
50 g/2 oz roasted hazelnuts, chopped
sliced banana and whole hazelnuts to decorate

Peel the bananas, place in a bowl and mash well with a fork. Beat in the lemon rind and juice and the rum. Add the yogurt and brown sugar and mix well.

Whisk the egg whites until they form stiff peaks and fold into the banana mixture. Put the bowl in the freezer and freeze until half frozen.

Remove from the freezer and whisk well. Stir in the chopped hazelnuts and return to the freezer to freeze again, until half frozen. Remove and stir well, taking care not to break up the nuts. Whisking and stirring the mixture while it is half frozen ensures a smooth, lump-free result. Spoon into a rigid container or serving dish and freeze until solid. Serve in scoops decorated with sliced banana and whole hazelnuts.

Raspberry and honey ice cream

———— SERVES 6 ————

450 g/1 lb fresh or frozen raspberries, thawed
1 tablespoon icing sugar, sifted
150 ml/¼ pint double cream
150 ml/¼ pint natural yogurt
2 tablespoons lemon juice
10 tablespoons clear honey
pinch of salt
3 egg whites
fresh raspberries to decorate

In an electric blender, purée the raspberries, sieve and sweeten with the icing sugar. Blend in the cream, yogurt, lemon juice, honey and salt. Pour the mixture into freezer trays and freeze until half frozen.

Meanwhile, whisk the egg whites until they stand in firm peaks. Whisk the half-frozen raspberry mixture until smooth, then fold in the egg whites. Return to the freezer and freeze again until half frozen. Whisk again until smooth, return to the freezer trays and freeze until firm. Serve the ice cream scooped into chilled glasses and decorate with fresh raspberries.

Brown bread ice cream

SERVES 4-6

300 ml/½ pint double cream
150 ml/¼ pint single cream
75 g/3 oz icing sugar, sifted
100 g/4 oz brown breadcrumbs
1 tablespoon dark rum (optional)
2 eggs, separated
sliced strawberries to decorate (optional)

This is a traditional English recipe for ice cream which is much more delicious than it sounds.

Whip the double cream until just stiff, then gradually whisk in the single cream. Fold in the icing sugar and breadcrumbs. Lightly beat the rum, if used, with the egg yolks and stir into the cream mixture.

Whisk the egg whites until they stand in stiff peaks and fold into the cream mixture. Pour the mixture into freezer trays or into a 1-litre/2-pint decorative ice cream mould and freeze for about 3-4 hours or until firm. Turn out and serve with sliced strawberries and crisp dessert biscuits.

Variation

Yogurt brown bread ice cream: Prepare as above but use 150 ml/¼ pint natural yogurt instead of the 150 ml/¼ pint single cream. This produces a sharper-flavoured ice cream.

Coffee granita

SERVES 4

600 ml/1 pint strong black coffee (made with
3 tablespoons freshly ground coffee or
4 tablespoons instant coffee granules)
75 g/3 oz castor sugar
chocolate leaves (page 122) and candied
coffee beans to decorate

Place the coffee and sugar in a saucepan and heat slowly until the sugar dissolves. Simmer for 5 minutes, cool, then pour into freezer trays. Freeze until half frozen, then transfer to a bowl and whisk until smooth. Return to the freezer trays and freeze until firm but not solid.

Serve the granita scooped into glasses and decorated with chocolate leaves and candied coffee beans.

Variation

Orange granita: Prepare as above but use 600 ml/1 pint fresh orange juice instead of the strong black coffee. Reduce the sugar content to 40 g/1½ oz. Serve decorated with orange slices (see page 00) and mint leaves.

Bombe cardinale

— SERVES 6 —

1 recipe Rich peach ice cream (page 98)
1 recipe Raspberry sorbet (page 98)
175 g/6 oz redcurrants, topped and tailed
2-3 tablespoons castor sugar
whipped cream and fresh redcurrants
to decorate

Place a 1.5-litre/2½-pint bombe mould or pudding basin in the freezer to chill.

Prepare the Rich peach ice cream and freeze until almost firm. When the ice cream is almost set, spoon over the base and sides of the chilled mould, forming a shell, and leaving the centre hollow. Build up the sides and base in stages if necessary. Freeze until firm, about 1-2 hours.

Meanwhile, prepare the Raspberry sorbet and when almost set, spoon on to the base and sides of the mould, over the peach ice cream, leaving a small hollow in the centre. Freeze until firm.

Meanwhile, poach the redcurrants in 50 ml/2 fl oz water for about 2-3 minutes. Drain but reserve the juice. In a saucepan, dissolve the sugar in the reserved redcurrant juice and bring to the boil. Simmer until a coating syrup is formed. Return the redcurrants to the syrup, stir and allow to cool. When cool, pour into the centre of the bombe and freeze until firm, about 2-4 hours.

To serve, dip the mould into warm water and turn out on to a serving plate. Decorate with whipped cream and fresh redcurrants.

Frozen Christmas pudding

— SERVES 6-8 —

350 g/12 oz mixed dried fruit
100 g/4 oz coloured glacé cherries, chopped
50 g/2 oz chopped mixed peel
50 g/2 oz flaked almonds
3 tablespoons sherry or dark rum
1 tablespoon cocoa powder, sifted
½ teaspoon mixed spice
1 egg, separated
50 g/2 oz icing sugar, sifted
300 ml/½ pint double cream
whipped cream, glacé cherries and angelica
to decorate

This is an excellent dessert for early Christmas parties but also proves a welcome alternative to the steaming hot variety on Christmas day.

Put the dried fruit, cherries, peel and almonds in a bowl and add the sherry or rum. Leave to soak for about 6 hours or overnight.

Add the cocoa powder to the fruit mixture with the spice and mix well. Add the egg yolk and icing sugar and beat until well combined. Whip the cream until it stands in soft peaks and fold into the fruit mixture. Whisk the egg white until it stands in firm peaks and fold into the cream mixture. Pour into a dampened 1-litre/2-pint pudding basin and freeze until firm, about 4-6 hours.

When ready to serve, dip the basin briefly into warm water and invert on to a serving dish. Leave for about 1 hour in the refrigerator so that the pudding softens a little. Decorate with whipped cream, glacé cherries and angelica. Top with a sprig of holly and cut into wedges to serve.

Frozen yogurt trifle

SERVES 4-6

about 16 sponge finger biscuits
3 tablespoons brandy or fresh orange juice
2 miniature jam rolls
600 ml/1 pint strawberry yogurt
8 macaroon biscuits, crushed
4 tablespoons raspberry jam
whipped cream and strawberries to decorate

Line the base of a 17.5-cm/7-inch charlotte mould with a piece of cooking foil. Dip the unsugared sides of the sponge fingers into the brandy or orange juice and line the sides of the mould, unsugared sides facing in. Slice the miniature jam rolls into rounds and line the base with them. Top with about one-third of the yogurt. Freeze until firm.

Top the yogurt with about half the macaroon crumbs and carefully spoon over half the jam. Pour over another one-third of the yogurt and freeze until firm. Repeat once more with the remaining macaroon crumbs, jam and yogurt. Freeze until firm, about 2-4 hours.

To serve, carefully turn out the trifle on to a serving plate, removing the cooking foil. Decorate with whipped cream and halved strawberries. Place in the refrigerator for about 1 hour to soften slightly before serving.

Mango or rhubarb parfait

SERVES 4-6

3 egg yolks
75 g/3 oz icing sugar, sifted
2 ripe mangoes, peeled, stoned and sieved *or*
175 g/6 oz thick rhubarb purée
(225 g/8 oz rhubarb cooked in 2 tablespoons
water, puréed or sieved)
1-2 teaspoons lemon juice
150 ml/¼ pint double cream
Chocolate curls (page 122) to decorate

Whisk the egg yolks lightly with the icing sugar and place in a bowl over a saucepan of barely simmering water. Cook, stirring, until the mixture is lukewarm, then remove from the heat. Whisk until cool then add the mango or rhubarb purée. Sweeten with extra sugar if necessary and add the lemon juice. Whip the cream until it stands in soft peaks then fold into the fruit mixture. Turn into parfait glasses or freezer-proof glasses and freeze until firm.

Remove the parfaits from the freezer and place in the refrigerator 1 hour before serving to soften slightly. Decorate with Chocolate curls.

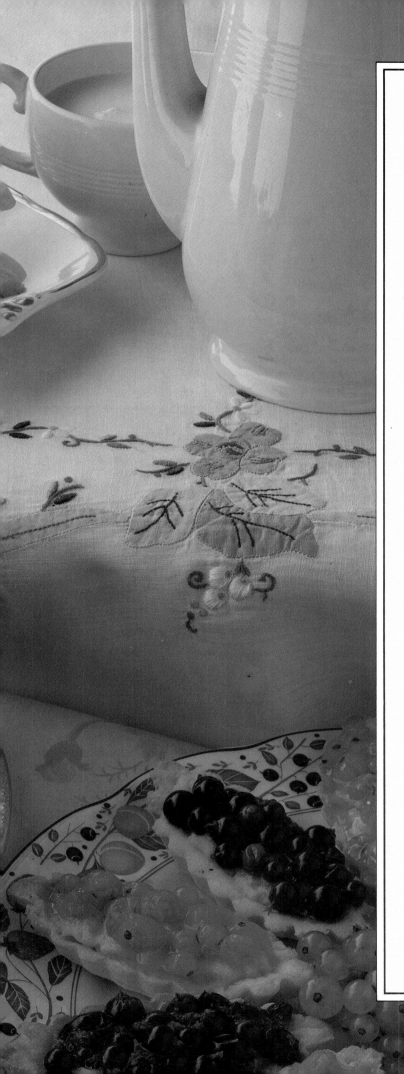

Bakers' delight

. . . mouth-watering gâteaux and cakes to make

Nothing can equal the flavour and aroma of a home-made cake, whether it be a simple Victoria sponge quickly prepared for a teatime treat or an elaborately decorated gâteau to toast a special celebration. Few puddings look as impressive as cakes and gâteaux, so use these recipes as the mainstay of your repertoire for entertaining, when the compliments really count!

Sadly, cakes and gâteaux are often the areas where people experience failure. Too wet a mixture producing a cavernous hollow in a heavy cake that should be light and airy; dry, crumbly fruit cake that is impossible to cut neatly or a cake that refuses to leave the tin in one piece are some of the more common failures. Lining tins carefully, weighing ingredients exactly and following recipes to the letter is the best advice for perfect results. Cake-making skills, however, are well worth the effort of learning.

If you're a beginner, then start with the simpler sponge recipes used in Harvest heart lemon cake, Cinnamon, apple and lemon torte and American carrot cake before advancing to Black Forest gâteau, Gâteau St Honoré and Gâteau Mount Pleasant. You'll find cake-making easy to master, exciting to do, and the results will be delicious to eat!

Black Forest gâteau, Shortcake gâteau and Soft fruit boats (overleaf)

Shortcake gâteau

275 g/10 oz plain flour
50 g/2 oz ground rice
100 g/4 oz castor sugar
finely grated rind of 1 lemon
225 g/8 oz butter
50 g/2 oz hazelnuts, skins removed and
finely chopped
1 egg yolk, beaten
300 ml/½ pint double cream
1 tablespoon icing sugar, sifted
450 g/1 lb fresh, frozen or canned raspberries or
loganberries, thawed or well drained

Grease a large baking tray. Sift the flour with the ground
rice into a bowl. Mix in the sugar and lemon rind. Cut the
butter into small pieces and add to the flour mixture. Rub
in with the fingertips until the mixture resembles fine
breadcrumbs. Add the hazelnuts, then mix to a soft
dough with the egg yolk and 3 tablespoons cold water.
Knead until the mixture forms a smooth ball, then wrap in
cooking foil and chill for 30 minutes.

Roll out two-thirds of the dough on a lightly floured
surface to make two 20 × 8.5-cm/8 × 3½-inch rectangles.
Roll out the remainder of the dough and cut out about
three circles with a 7.5-cm/3-inch fluted biscuit cutter.
Cut each circle in half to form 6 semicircles. Place the
rectangles and semicircles on the prepared baking tray
and cook in a moderate oven (180 C, 350 F, Gas Mark 4) for
20-25 minutes. Cool on a wire rack.

To assemble, whip the cream with the icing sugar until
it forms soft peaks. Place in a piping bag fitted with a star-
shaped nozzle and pipe about half the cream on to one of
the shortcake rectangles. Top with the fruit, reserving a
few whole berries for decoration. Cover with the
remaining shortcake rectangle. Pipe swirls of cream down
the centre of the rectangle and arrange the shortcake
semicircles along the cream. Decorate the top with the
reserved whole berries. Serve within 2 hours.

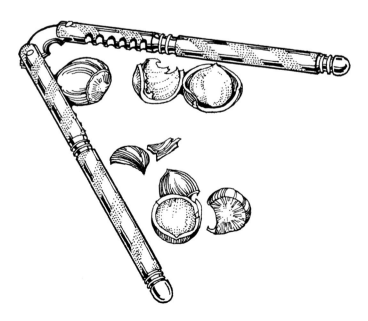

Black Forest gâteau

2 (425-g/15-oz) cans Morello cherries
8 tablespoons Kirsch
CAKE
6 eggs
225 g/8 oz castor sugar
½ teaspoon vanilla essence
75 g/3 oz plain flour
50 g/2 oz cocoa powder
100 g/4 oz butter, melted
maraschino cherries to decorate
75 g/3 oz Chocolate curls (page 122) or
grated chocolate
FILLING
450 ml/¾ pint double cream
50 g/2 oz icing sugar, sifted
50 g/2 oz plain chocolate, grated

Grease and flour a 23-cm/9-inch round cake tin. Drain the
cherries and place in a bowl with 5 tablespoons of the
Kirsch. Leave to macerate for at least 2 hours.

Place the eggs, sugar and vanilla in a large bowl. Place
the bowl over a saucepan of barely simmering water and
whisk until very thick. Remove from the heat and whisk
until cool. Sift the flour and cocoa powder together and
fold into the egg mixture. Using a metal spoon, fold in the
melted butter, taking care not to lose too much air. Pour
into the prepared tin and bake in a moderately hot oven
(190 C, 375 F, Gas Mark 5) for about 40-60 minutes, or
until well risen and firm to touch. Allow to cool in the tin
slightly then turn out to cool on a wire rack. When cool,
split horizontally into three layers.

Drain the cherries with a slotted spoon and sprinkle the
cake layers with the Kirsch-flavoured juice. To make the
filling, whip the cream with the icing sugar and
remaining Kirsch until it stands in soft peaks. Fold the
cherries into half of the cream and use to sandwich the
cake layers together. Spread two-thirds of the remaining
cream around the sides and on the top of the cake.
Decorate the sides of the cake with the grated chocolate,
pressing gently to secure.

Pipe or spoon the remaining cream in swirls on top of
the cake and decorate with maraschino cherries. Fill the
centre of the gâteau with the Chocolate curls or extra
grated chocolate. Chill lightly before serving.

Variation

Black Forest gâteau with confectioner's custard:
Black Forest gâteau is all the more delicious if filled with
confectioner's custard. Mix 2 egg yolks with 20 g/¾ oz
sugar, 20 g/¾ oz flour, 15 g/½ oz cornflour and a little milk
from 300 ml/½ pint. Boil the remaining milk, pour on to
the egg mixture and mix well. Return to the saucepan and
cook until smooth and thickened. Allow to cool. Whisk 1
egg white until stiff with 40 g/1½ oz castor sugar. Fold into
the cooled mixture and use as required.

Soft fruit boats

MAKES 12-14

175 g/6 oz redcurrants, topped and tailed
175 g/6 oz blackcurrants, topped and tailed
100 g/4 oz castor sugar
2 teaspoons arrowroot blended with a
little water
PASTRY BOATS
100 g/4 oz plain flour
pinch of salt
50 g/2 oz castor sugar
50 g/2 oz butter, softened
2 egg yolks
$\frac{1}{2}$ recipe Confectioner's custard (opposite page)

Place the fruit and the sugar in a saucepan with 2 tablespoons water. Bring to the boil and add the arrowroot. Stirring continuously, cook until clear and thickened. Allow to cool.

Prepare the pastry by sifting the flour and the salt together in a bowl. Stir in the sugar, butter and egg yolks to form a firm dough. Roll out on a lightly floured board or work surface and use to line 12-14 boat-shaped tins or barquette moulds. Prick the bases with a fork and bake blind (see page 119) for 5-7 minutes. Remove the paper and beans or cooking foil and cook for a further 2-3 minutes. Remove the pastry boats from their tins and cool on a wire rack.

When cool, fill the boats with the cooled confectioner's custard and top with the cool, thickened fruit. Chill and serve on day of making.

Aladdin's cave gâteau

SERVES 6-8

CAKE
4 eggs
100 g/4 oz castor sugar
100 g/4 oz self-raising flour
$\frac{1}{4}$ teaspoon salt
FILLING
300 ml/$\frac{1}{2}$ pint double cream, whipped
2 teaspoons castor sugar
350 g/12 oz prepared soft fruits (for example,
raspberries, redcurrants and blackcurrants)
25 g/1 oz icing sugar, sifted
a few fruits with stems for decoration

Grease and flour a 35×20-cm/14×8-inch rectangular cake tin. Place the eggs and sugar in a bowl. Place the bowl over a saucepan of hot water and whisk until thick. Remove from the heat and whisk until cool. Sift the flour and salt together and, using a metal spoon, fold into the egg mixture. Pour into the prepared cake tin and bake in a moderately hot oven (190 C, 375 F, Gas Mark 5) for 15 minutes, or until well risen and golden. Allow to cool on a wire rack.

Carefully cut the sponge vertically in half and spread the bottom layer with the whipped cream. Sprinkle with the castor sugar. Carefully position the second sponge layer on top of the cream at an angle so that its edge rests on the side of the plate and it looks like an open jewellery box. Fill the open sponge and cream centre with the prepared fruit, allowing it to spill over the edge of the cake. Chill lightly before serving.

Sponge finger pavé

SERVES 4-6

50 g/2 oz castor sugar
3 tablespoons rum
18 sponge fingers
100 g/4 oz plain chocolate
100 g/4 oz butter
100 g/4 oz icing sugar, sifted
4 egg yolks
Chocolate curls (page 122) and desiccated
coconut to decorate

Dissolve the sugar in 3 tablespoons water and bring to the boil. Remove from the heat and add the rum. Dip the sponge fingers lightly in this syrup, set aside, then reduce any remaining syrup over a high heat until thick.

Melt the chocolate in a bowl over a saucepan of hot water. Cream the butter and icing sugar until light and fluffy. Beat in the egg yolks then stir in the melted chocolate. Beat in the cooled, thick syrup.

To assemble the pavé, divide the sponge fingers into three portions. Arrange a neat row of six on the base of a serving dish. Spread with a layer of the chocolate mixture. Add a second layer of sponge fingers and chocolate cream. Top with the final layer of sponge fingers. Use the remaining chocolate cream to cover the top and sides of the pavé. Decorate the sides with the Chocolate curls and the top with desiccated coconut. Chill for at least 6 hours or overnight, then slice diagonally to serve attractive striped slices of cake.

Gâteau Mount Pleasant

SERVES 6-8

100 g/4 oz castor sugar
4 eggs
100 g/4 oz plain flour
100 g/4 oz butter, melted
675 g/1½ lb cooking apples, peeled, cored
and sliced
½ teaspoon ground cinnamon
2 tablespoons Calvados
TOPPING
2 dessert apples
1 tablespoon sugar
juice of ½ lemon
3 tablespoons apricot jam
300 ml/½ pint whipping cream
½ teaspoon ground cinnamon

Grease and flour a 20-cm/8-inch round cake tin. Place the sugar and eggs in a bowl and whisk until thick. Place the bowl over a saucepan of simmering water and whisk until very thick. Remove from the heat and continue to whisk until cool. Carefully fold in the flour and butter using a metal spoon. Pour into the prepared tin and bake in a moderately hot oven (200 C, 400 F, Gas Mark 6) for about 35 minutes or until cooked; cool.

Meanwhile, cook the apples in a saucepan with the cinnamon and about 2 tablespoons water to form a thick purée. Cool. Slice the cake horizontally into three layers and sprinkle the bottom and middle layer with the Calvados. Sandwich together using the apple purée.

For the topping, core and slice but do not peel the apples. Poach in a little water with the sugar and lemon juice until soft but still firm in shape. Drain and cool. Arrange the apple slices decoratively on top of the gâteau. Warm the apricot jam and brush over the apple slices. Whip the cream with the cinnamon and spoon or pipe decoratively around the cake.

Walnut and strawberry galette

SERVES 6

GALETTE
175 g/6 oz butter or margarine
100 g/4 oz castor sugar
grated rind of ½ lemon
175 g/6 oz plain flour
100 g/4 oz walnuts, roughly chopped
FILLING
300 ml/½ pint whipping cream
1 tablespoon icing sugar
675 g/1½ lb strawberries, hulled
a few strawberries with stalks to decorate

Grease three baking trays. Cream the butter or margarine and sugar together until light and fluffy. Beat in the lemon rind and fold in the flour. Knead until smooth and chill for 30 minutes.

Divide the dough into three portions and roll each portion out on a lightly floured board or work surface to a 17.5-cm/7-inch circle. Pinch the edges of the circles to form a decorative shape. Place on to the prepared baking trays and sprinkle the top of each with the chopped nuts, pressing gently to secure. Bake in a moderate oven (180 C, 350 F, Gas Mark 4) for 20-25 minutes or until golden. Allow to cool slightly on the trays, then transfer to cool on a wire rack.

To make the filling, whip the cream with the icing sugar until it stands in soft peaks. Slice 450 g/1 lb of the strawberries and fold into two-thirds of the cream. Use to sandwich the rounds together. Pipe or spoon the remaining cream in swirls on top of the galette and decorate with the remaining whole, stalked strawberries. Chill for 30 minutes before serving.

Honey walnut roulade

SERVES 4-6

ROULADE
3 large eggs, separated
2 teaspoons water
75 g/3 oz castor sugar
2 tablespoons clear honey
100 g/4 oz self-raising flour, sifted
75 g/3 oz ground walnuts
castor sugar to sprinkle
FILLING
150 ml/¼ pint double cream
25 g/1 oz walnut pieces
1 tablespoon clear honey
whipped cream and walnut halves to decorate

Line a 24 × 28-cm/9½ × 11-inch Swiss roll tin with greaseproof paper. Grease liberally and dust with a little flour.

Whisk the egg whites with the water until very stiff. Gradually add the sugar, a spoonful at a time, whisking until thick and glossy. Whisk in the egg yolks and honey, then, using a metal spoon, carefully fold in the flour and ground walnuts. Turn the mixture carefully into the prepared tin and level off the top. Bake in a moderately hot oven (200 C, 400 F, Gas Mark 6) for 12-14 minutes.

When cooked, turn out quickly on to a sheet of greaseproof paper sprinkled with a little sugar. Trim away the edges of the roll with a sharp knife and roll up, from the short end, like a Swiss roll, keeping the greaseproof paper inside. Leave until cold.

Meanwhile, to make the filling, whip the cream until thick and fold in the walnut pieces and honey. Unroll the roulade and carefully remove the greaseproof paper. Spread with the cream mixture and re-roll. Dust with a little extra sugar and decorate with whipped cream and walnut halves.

Ice cream coffee gâteau

— SERVES 6 —

2 tablespoons apricot jam
10 sponge fingers, halved
2 eggs, separated
2 tablespoons coffee essence
1 tablespoon medium dry sherry
4 tablespoons icing sugar
150 ml/¼ pint double cream
grated chocolate and whipped cream to decorate

Gently heat the jam and brush the edges of the biscuits. Use to line the sides of a 15-cm/6-inch round cake tin lined with greaseproof paper. Stand the biscuits around the edge, sugared sides facing out, pressing the biscuits close together.

Beat the egg yolks with the coffee essence and sherry. Whisk the egg whites until they stand in firm peaks. Gradually whisk in the icing sugar and continue to whisk until thick and glossy. Fold into the coffee and egg yolk mixture. Whip the cream until it stands in soft peaks and fold into the coffee mixture. Pour into the prepared tin and freeze until firm, about 6 hours.

To serve, turn out on to a chilled serving dish and decorate with grated chocolate and whipped cream.

American carrot cake

— SERVES 8 —

CARROT CAKE
225 g/8 oz butter
225 g/8 oz castor sugar
4 eggs, beaten
225 g/8 oz self-raising flour
grated rind of 1 lemon
2 tablespoons lemon juice
1 tablespoon Kirsch
225 g/8 oz carrots, peeled and grated
100 g/4 oz blanched almonds, finely chopped
LEMON ICING
225 g/8 oz icing sugar, sifted
5 teaspoons lemon juice
marzipan and angelica to decorate

Grease and line a 20-cm/8-inch round cake tin with greaseproof paper. Cream the butter and sugar together until light and fluffy. Beat in the eggs with a little of the flour, then fold in the remaining flour with the lemon rind and juice and Kirsch. Add the carrots and almonds and mix well to blend. Turn into the prepared tin and bake in a moderate oven (180 C, 350 F, Gas Mark 4) for 1½ hours or until well risen, golden and firm to the touch. Turn out and cool on a wire rack.

To make the icing, mix the icing sugar with the lemon juice until smooth and glossy. Pour over the top of the cooled cake, allowing a little of the icing to run down the sides. Decorate with marzipan (coloured orange, if liked) shaped into carrots with green angelica tops.

Cinnamon, apple and lemon torte

— SERVES 6 —

175 g/6 oz butter or margarine
175 g/6 oz soft light brown sugar
75 g/3 oz oat flakes
1 teaspoon ground cinnamon
450 g/1 lb cooking apples, peeled, cored
and sliced
grated rind and juice of 1 lemon
2 eggs, beaten
100 g/4 oz self-raising flour
1 teaspoon ground mixed spice
150 ml/$\frac{1}{4}$ pint whipping cream, whipped
3 tablespoons apricot jam, warmed

Grease and line the base of a 19-cm/7$\frac{1}{2}$-inch round cake tin with greaseproof paper. Melt 50 g/2 oz of the butter in a heavy-based saucepan and fry 50 g/2 oz of the sugar with the oats and cinnamon until golden. Spoon into the prepared tin and level the top.

Mix the apple with the lemon rind and juice. Cream the remaining butter and sugar together until light and fluffy. Gradually beat in the eggs. Sift the flour with the mixed spice and fold into the egg mixture. Finally fold in the prepared apple. Spoon into the tin on top of the oat mixture and level the top. Bake in a moderate oven (180 C, 350 F, Gas Mark 4) for about 50 minutes. Turn out on to a serving dish and allow to cool.

To serve, top the torte with the whipped cream and spoon or pipe lines of jam across the cake. Swirl through the cake, if liked.

Strawberry choux gâteau

— SERVES 6-8 —

1 recipe Choux pastry (page 81)
15 g/$\frac{1}{2}$ oz blanched almonds
icing sugar, sifted, to sprinkle
300 ml/$\frac{1}{2}$ pint double cream
juice of $\frac{1}{2}$ lemon
25 g/1 oz castor sugar
225 g/8 oz strawberries, hulled
a few fruits with stalks for decoration

Lightly grease and flour a baking tray. Mark out a 17.5-cm/7-inch circle. Spoon the prepared choux pastry into a piping bag fitted with a 2-cm/$\frac{3}{4}$-inch plain nozzle and pipe a circle of pastry on to the tray using the marked circle as a guide. Pipe another circle of pastry on top of the first. Sprinkle with the almonds and bake in a moderately hot oven (200 C, 400 F, Gas Mark 6) for 15 minutes. Sprinkle with a little icing sugar and reduce the heat to moderately hot (190 C, 375 F, Gas Mark 5) and cook for a further 35-40 minutes.

Immediately the ring is removed from the oven, split it in half horizontally and scoop out and discard any uncooked pastry. Return the halves to the oven and cook for a further 5 minutes to dry out. Allow to cool.

Whip the cream until it stands in soft peaks. Stir in the lemon juice and the castor sugar. Chop all but about eight of the strawberries and fold into the cream. Use this cream and fruit mixture to sandwich the choux rings together. Decorate with the reserved strawberries. Dust with a little icing sugar before serving, if liked.

Harvest heart lemon cake

SERVES 6

275 g/10 oz butter or margarine
275 g/10 oz castor sugar
5 eggs, beaten
275 g/10 oz self-raising flour
grated rind of 2 lemons
15 g/½ oz angelica
25 g/1 oz glacé cherries, chopped
15 g/½ oz flaked almonds
100 g/4 oz butter
225 g/8 oz icing sugar
2 tablespoons lemon juice

Grease and line the base of a deep 20-cm/8-inch heart-shaped tin with greaseproof paper. Cream the butter and sugar together until fluffy. Beat in the eggs with the flour and lemon rind. Place in the prepared tin and bake in a moderate oven (180 C, 350 F, Gas Mark 4) for about 1½ hours. Turn out and cool on a wire rack.

Cut the cake into two layers. To make the filling, cream the butter with the icing sugar and lemon juice. Pipe on to the bottom layer and cover with the top layer. Sprinkle with angelica, cherries and almonds.

Brandy snap creams

MAKES ABOUT 20

50 g/2 oz butter or margarine
1 tablespoon golden syrup
50 g/2 oz soft brown sugar
1 teaspoon lemon juice
50 g/2 oz plain flour
1 teaspoon ground ginger
½ teaspoon ground mixed spice
300 ml/½ pint double cream
25 g/1 oz very finely chopped stem ginger
1 teaspoon brandy or ginger wine (optional)
2 tablespoons chopped mixed nuts

Melt the fat in a pan with the golden syrup and sugar. When bubbling, add the lemon juice, flour, ginger and mixed spice, mixing well. Place teaspoonfuls on to a greased baking tray, allowing room for the snaps to spread. Bake in batches in a moderate oven (180 C, 350 F, Gas Mark 4) for 6-8 minutes. Cool slightly, lift with a spatula and while hot, mould around cream horn tins or the greased handles of wooden spoons. Cool, then remove from the moulds.

Whip the cream with the stem ginger and brandy or ginger wine if used. Fill the brandy snaps and dip the ends into the nuts. Chill slightly before serving.

Chocolate éclairs

1 recipe Choux pastry (page 81)
1 recipe Confectioner's custard (page 106)
or 300 ml/½ pint double cream, whipped
225 g/8 oz plain dessert chocolate, melted

Prepare the choux pastry according to the recipe instructions and spoon the mixture into a piping bag fitted with a 1-cm/½-inch plain nozzle. Pipe 9-cm/3½-inch fingers on to a baking tray, allowing a little space between each for rising during baking. Bake in a moderately hot oven (200 c, 400 f, Gas Mark 6) for about 30-35 minutes. Remove from the oven and immediately slit with a knife to allow any steam to escape.

When the éclairs are cold, cut a lid from each one and fill with the cold confectioner's custard or, alternatively, fill with whipped cream. Melt the chocolate and spread over the top of each éclair with a palette knife. Serve the éclairs slightly chilled.

Marie-Louise cakes

100 g/4 oz plain chocolate
50 g/2 oz sponge cake, crumbled
75 g/3 oz prepared soft fruit (for example,
raspberries, strawberries or cherries)
2-3 tablespoons sherry
300 ml/½ pint double cream
crystallised fruit or flowers to decorate

Melt the chocolate in a bowl over a saucepan of hot water. Use the melted chocolate to coat the insides of seven paper baking cases, then turn the cases upside down so that the chocolate edges remain thicker than the base. Chill until set. When well chilled, carefully peel off the paper cases.

Fill the chocolate cups with the crumbled sponge cake mixed with the fruit. Sprinkle with sherry to moisten. Whip the cream until it stands in soft peaks, then pipe or spoon generously into the chocolate cups. Serve chilled, decorated with crystallised fruit or flowers.

Gâteau St Honoré

SERVES 4-6

100 g/4 oz plain flour
pinch of salt
75 g/3 oz butter
1 recipe Choux pastry (page 81)
12 sugar cubes
$\frac{1}{2}$ recipe Confectioner's custard, cooled
(page 106)
450 ml/$\frac{3}{4}$ pint whipping cream
50 g/2 oz vanilla sugar (page 36)
glacé cherries, angelica and crystallised violets
to decorate

Grease two baking trays. Mix the flour and salt together in a bowl. Rub in the butter until the mixture resembles fine breadcrumbs. Mix in 2-3 tablespoons water to form a stiff dough. Roll out on a lightly floured board or work surface to form a 15-cm/6-inch circle. Place on the baking tray.

Prepare the choux pastry according to the recipe instructions and spoon into a piping bag fitted with a 1.5-cm/$\frac{1}{2}$-inch plain nozzle. Pipe small buns around the edge of the pastry circle, about 2.5 cm/1 inch in from the edge. Pipe the remaining choux pastry into buns of the same size on to the second baking tray. Bake both trays in a moderately hot oven (200 c, 400 f, Gas Mark 6) for 15-20 minutes or until well risen and golden brown. Allow to cool.

Heat the sugar cubes in a saucepan with 2 tablespoons water until dissolved. Boil briskly to form a golden caramel. Dip the separate choux buns in the caramel and position on top of the layer of buns on the pastry.

Spoon the cooled confectioner's custard into the centre base of the gâteau. Whip the cream with the vanilla sugar until it stands in soft peaks. Pipe or spoon on top of the confectioner's custard. Decorate with glacé cherries, angelica and crystallised violets.

Mocha brandy cake

SERVES 6-8

CAKE
175 g/6 oz plain flour
2 teaspoons baking powder
$\frac{1}{2}$ teaspoon salt
150 g/5 oz soft brown sugar
2 eggs, separated
6 tablespoons corn oil
4 tablespoons milk
1 tablespoon cocoa powder
1 tablespoon coffee essence
GLAZE
100 g/4 oz granulated sugar
5 tablespoons strong black coffee
1 tablespoon cocoa powder
2 tablespoons brandy
300 ml/$\frac{1}{2}$ pint double cream,
whipped, and 25 g/1 oz toasted flaked almonds
to decorate

Grease and flour a shallow 20-cm/8-inch cake tin. Sift the flour, baking powder and salt together in a bowl and mix in the sugar. Add the egg yolks, oil, milk, cocoa powder and coffee essence together and beat into the flour. Whisk the egg whites until they stand in firm peaks and fold into the flour mixture with a metal spoon. Pour into the prepared cake tin and bake in a moderate oven (180 c, 350 f, Gas Mark 4) for about 45 minutes. Allow to cool slightly in the tin, then turn out to cool on a wire rack.

For the glaze, place the sugar, black coffee, cocoa powder and 4 tablespoons water in a saucepan. Heat to dissolve then bring to the boil and simmer for 5 minutes. Remove from the heat and add the brandy. Prick all over the surface of the cake with a skewer and place it back in the tin. Pour over the hot syrup and leave to soak. To serve, top the cake with the whipped cream and almonds.

114

Sachertorte

SERVES 6-8

100 g/4 oz butter
175 g/6 oz castor sugar
175 g/6 oz plain chocolate, melted
1 teaspoon vanilla essence
6 egg yolks
75 g/3 oz plain flour
8 egg whites
6 tablespoons apricot jam, warmed
CHOCOLATE ICING
225 g/8 oz plain chocolate
100 ml/4 fl oz double cream
350 g/12 oz icing sugar, sifted
whipped cream and chocolate curls to decorate

Grease and flour a 23-cm/9-inch loose-bottomed cake tin. Cream the butter and sugar together until light and fluffy. Beat in the melted chocolate and vanilla. Gradually add the egg yolks with a little of the flour, then fold in the remaining flour. Whisk the egg whites until they stand in firm peaks and fold into the chocolate mixture. Spoon into the prepared tin and bake in a moderate oven (180 C, 350 F, Gas Mark 4) for 50-60 minutes. Leave to cool in the tin for 30 minutes, then cool on a wire rack.

Slice the cake in half horizontally and sandwich together with the warmed apricot jam.

For the icing, melt the chocolate in a bowl over a saucepan of hot water. Beat in the cream and icing sugar. Allow to cool for 10 minutes, then spread over the top and sides of the cake. A smooth finish can be achieved if a wet palette knife is used to finish the icing. Leave to set for about 30 minutes. Decorate with swirls of whipped cream and chocolate curls before serving.

Gâteau Pithiviers

SERVES 6

1 (398-g/14-oz) packet frozen puff pastry, thawed
100 g/4 oz ground almonds
100 g/4 oz castor sugar
40 g/1½ oz unsalted butter, melted
2 egg yolks
2 tablespoons double cream
2 tablespoons dark rum
beaten egg to glaze
1 tablespoon icing sugar, sifted

Roll out the pastry on a lightly floured surface to form two 23-cm/9-inch circles. Line a 20-cm/8-inch pie plate with one of the circles.

Cream together the almonds, sugar, butter, egg yolks, cream and rum. Spoon into the prepared pie plate. Brush the pastry rim with water and top with the second pastry circle. Press the edges together firmly to seal. Decorate the top with any trimmings.

Using a sharp knife, make about 12 v-shaped cuts around the edge of the gâteau. Using your fingers, push up the pastry at each cut to form petal shapes. Glaze with beaten egg and bake in a hot oven (230 C, 450 F, Gas Mark 8) for 10-15 minutes. Reduce the heat to moderately hot (200 C, 400 F, Gas Mark 6) for a further 20-30 minutes, or until golden and cooked through.

Remove from the oven, dust with the icing sugar and place briefly under a hot grill to caramelise the sugar. Serve the gâteau warm with single cream or natural yogurt.

Raspberry chocolate box

CAKE
4 eggs, beaten
100 g/4 oz castor sugar
grated rind of ½ lemon
75 g/3 oz plain flour
25 g/1 oz cornflour
50 g/2 oz butter, melted
FILLING
900 g/2 lb raspberries, hulled
juice of 2 oranges
2 tablespoons Cointreau or Grand Marnier
(optional)
450 ml/¾ pint double cream
1 tablespoon icing sugar (optional)
CHOCOLATE BOX
175 g/6 oz plain chocolate, grated

Grease and flour a 20-cm/8-inch square cake tin. Place the eggs, sugar and lemon rind in a large bowl. Place over a saucepan of barely simmering water and whisk until thick. Remove from the heat and continue to whisk until cool. Sift the flour and cornflour together and fold into the egg mixture with a metal spoon. Carefully fold in the melted butter, taking care not to lose too much air. Bake in a moderately hot oven (190 C, 375 F, Gas Mark 5) for 30-35 minutes or until the cake is well risen, golden and firm to the touch. Allow to cool slightly in the tin then turn out to cool on a wire rack.

Split the cooled cake horizontally into three layers. Reserve about one-third of the raspberries for the top decoration. Sprinkle the bottom and middle layer of the cake with the orange juice and Cointreau or Grand Marnier, if used. Whip the cream until it stands in soft peaks and, reserving a little for the sides, fold the remaining raspberries into it. Use the cream and raspberry filling to sandwich the three layers of the cake together and spread the rest of the cream around the sides.

Carefully position the reserved raspberries on top of the cake and dust with a little icing sugar, if liked. Melt the chocolate in a bowl over a saucepan of hot water and spread into a thin layer over greaseproof paper, using a palette knife. When cold, cut into squares slightly taller than the cake and place them, overlapping slightly, along the sides of the cake to form a 'chocolate box'. Chill lightly before serving.

Redcurrant and blackcurrant roulade

ROULADE
3 large eggs, separated
100 g/4 oz castor sugar
grated rind and juice of ½ lemon
50 g/2 oz fine semolina
1 tablespoon ground almonds
castor sugar to sprinkle
FILLING
150 ml/¼ pint whipping cream
75 g/3 oz redcurrants, topped and tailed
75 g/3 oz blackcurrants, topped and tailed
1 tablespoon icing sugar, sifted (optional)
whipped cream, redcurrants and blackcurrants
to decorate

Line a 24 × 28-cm/9½ × 11-inch Swiss roll tin with greaseproof paper. Grease liberally and dust with a little castor sugar and flour.

Whisk the egg yolks with the sugar until pale and thick. Beat in the lemon rind and juice. Using a metal spoon, carefully fold in the semolina and ground almonds. Whisk the egg whites until they stand in firm peaks, then carefully fold through the almond mixture. Turn the mixture carefully into the prepared tin and level off the top. Bake in a moderate oven (180 C, 350 F, Gas Mark 4) for 25-30 minutes or until just firm to touch.

When cooked, turn out quickly on to a sheet of greaseproof paper sprinkled with a little sugar. Trim away the edges of the roll with a sharp knife and roll up from the short end, like a Swiss roll, with the greaseproof paper inside. Leave until cold.

Meanwhile, to make the filling, whip the cream until it stands in firm peaks then fold in the prepared redcurrants and blackcurrants. Sweeten with the icing sugar, if liked. Unroll the roulade and remove the greaseproof paper. The roulade may crack a little, but this is typical of the dessert. Spread with the cream and fruit mixture and re-roll. Decorate with whipped cream and washed redcurrants and blackcurrants.

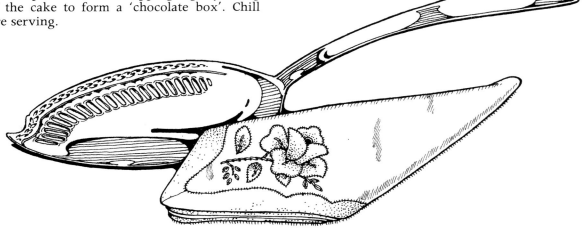

Guidelines for good results

The secret of a successful pudding or dessert often lies in the basic preparation, whether it be a perfectly whisked meringue for a pie topping or a carefully lined tin for a gâteau. If you follow the tips given for some of the more frequently used basic techniques found in this book you will achieve first-class results time and time again.

Lining a pudding basin with suet-crust pastry

Roll out the pastry on a lightly floured board or work surface to form a circle large enough to line the basin used – about 30 cm/12 inches in diameter for a 2-pint pudding basin. Remove one quarter segment of the pastry circle and reserve for the lid. Lift the remaining piece of dough and ease into the basin, pinching the two uncut edges together to seal and moulding the dough into the base and around the sides of the basin. Add the filling. Roll the reserved pastry into a circle large enough to top the basin and brush the edges lightly with water. Place over the basin and pinch the damp edges together to secure. Trim away any excess pastry and cover with greased grease-proof paper and a piece of cooking foil pleated to allow for expansion. Tie securely with string and steam for the time directed in the recipe.

Christmas pudding and Sussex pond pudding (page 87)

118

Lining a shallow cake tin

Place the cake tin on a piece of greaseproof paper and mark the paper around the edge with a pencil. Cut out the circle of paper to line the base of the tin. Grease the bottom and sides of the tin with a little melted butter or oil and lay the paper circle on to the base. Brush the paper with a little more melted butter or oil. Dust the sides of the tin and paper with flour until the surface is lightly coated. Tip away any excess flour and use the tin as required.

Lining a flan tin

Roll out the pastry thinly on a lightly floured board or work surface. Lift by rolling the pastry loosely around the rolling pin, lay it over the flan tin and let it unroll. Ease the pastry carefully into the corners of the flan tin, avoiding any stretching. Roll the rolling pin over the top of the flan to remove any excess pastry. Press the pastry in to the shape of the flan tin and pinch it slightly at the top, raising it above the edge to allow for shrinkage. Leave to rest for 30 minutes. Line the pastry with cooking foil or greaseproof paper and beans if baking 'blind'.

Baking 'blind'

To prevent the bottom crust of a pie or quiche from becoming soggy or remaining rather undercooked, it is a good idea to bake the pastry 'blind' before adding the filling. You can cook the pastry case either partially or completely, the choice depending upon the filling you intend to use. If the filling has to be cooked, then it is best to pre-bake the pastry, adding the filling just before the pastry is cooked and continuing the cooking with the filling. If, however, you do not need to cook the filling, then you can bake the pastry case completely.

Use dried beans, cooking foil, rice, pasta or a smaller tin of the same shape to weigh down the pastry so that it does not buckle up as it cooks.

Line a pie plate or flan tin with the pastry. Cut a square of cooking foil or greaseproof paper slightly larger than the flan tin and use it to line the base and sides. Weigh down with beans, pasta or rice if greaseproof paper is used. Bake in a moderately hot oven (200 C, 400 F, Gas Mark 6) for 10-15 minutes. Remove the paper and beans or cooking foil and bake for a further 5 minutes. Add the filling if this needs cooking, then follow the specific recipe instructions. If a completely baked pastry case is required, then bake for a further 15 minutes after removing the paper and beans or cooking foil.

119

Dissolving gelatine

Gelatine needs careful preparation before use in pudding and dessert recipes. Ideally, sprinkle the gelatine into a little water in a small bowl placed in a saucepan of hot water and stir until the gelatine is completely dissolved and the water is clear. Never sprinkle gelatine into hot liquid or it will probably go lumpy and give a stringy texture to the end result.

Chilling a gelatine mixture: Often it is necessary to chill a gelatine mixture until it becomes syrupy before adding any extra ingredients. It is possible to speed up this sometimes time-consuming method by placing the bowl containing the gelatine mixture in a dish of crushed ice. The mixture is ready if the gelatine forms a mound when dropped from a spoon on to a clean plate.

Making a 'collar' for a soufflé dish

Cut a wide strip of cooking foil or greaseproof paper, long enough to wrap around the soufflé dish with a 5-cm/ 2-inch overlap. Fold the cooking foil or paper in half lengthways to double the strength.

Wrap it around the dish so that it stands about 7.5 cm/ 3 inches above the rim and secure tightly with string.

To remove, ease the soufflé carefully away from the cooking foil or paper with a knife dipped in hot water.

Turning out moulded desserts

Loosen a dessert from its mould by carefully running a palette knife around the top edge of the dish. Dip the dish quickly into hot water for a few seconds. Invert it on to a dampened plate (this enables you to reposition the dessert later if not central) and, holding the mould firmly on the plate, carefully shake the pudding from its mould. Lift off the mould and reposition the dessert by sliding gently, if necessary.

Whisking a perfect meringue

Separate the eggs and place the whites in a clean, oil-free bowl. Reserve the yolks for other dishes. Using a clean, oil-free whisk, beat the whites with a regular figure-of-eight motion. When the whites begin to form soft peaks, gradually add half the castor sugar. Continue to whisk until the egg white forms stiff peaks and the meringue becomes firm and glossy. Fold in the remaining sugar with a metal spoon. Use at once.

Decorative touches

Suitable decorations for puddings and desserts add good looks as well as flavour. But remember, they must be fresh and complement the pudding or dessert they adorn. Colours should be chosen to tone with both the food and its setting or serving dish, and flavours should complement the pudding or dessert base and the filling or topping. Here are a few guidelines to follow to make some of the more elaborate decorations used in this book.

Decorative pastry edges

Forked edge: Press a floured fork around the outer edge of the pastry rim.

Fluted edge: Using thumb and forefinger, pinch the pastry together to make curved flutes.

Rope edge: Press your thumb into the pastry edge at an angle and pinch the pastry between it and the knuckle of your index finger. Repeat this all the way round, remembering to place your thumb each time in the indentation made by the index finger.

Scalloped edge: Place your thumb and forefinger about 3 cm/1¼ inches apart on the outside of the pastry edge and press the pastry outwards between them. Repeat, pinching the points between the scallops.

Cut edge: Make small cuts about 1 cm/½ inch deep at 1-cm/½-inch intervals around the pastry edge. Fold in the cuts at alternate intervals and press down firmly to secure.

Scoring a soufflé or sweet omelette

For a really professional look, dredge an omelette or sweet soufflé with sifted icing sugar just before serving. To score a criss-cross pattern across the top, thoroughly but carefully heat a skewer until red hot over a gas flame. Press on to the sugar which will caramelise to produce an attractive pattern.

Sweetening whipped cream

Pour 300 ml/½ pint whipping or double cream into a bowl and add sugar to taste. Whip the cream with a balloon whisk or electric beater until the mixture begins to thicken and forms soft peaks. Use at once or cover with cling film or cooking foil and store in the refrigerator for up to 1 hour.

Frosting grapes

Dip a small bunch of grapes, still on their stalk, into a little beaten egg white to coat thoroughly, then quickly dip into a little castor sugar. Leave to dry on a wire rack before using.

Jamaican jelly creams (page 28) and Tropical ginger and orange trifle (page 29)

Chocolate decorations

Chocolate leaves: Spread melted chocolate thinly on to greaseproof paper. When firm but not brittle, cut out leaf shapes using a sharp knife. Leave to harden, then ease them away from the paper. Alternatively, dip in melted chocolate the underside of washed and very lightly oiled rose leaves. Leave to harden, then carefully peel away the leaf from the chocolate.

Chocolate curls or scrolls: Spread melted chocolate on to a hard, even surface such as a marble slab or baking tray. Spread out with a palette knife to the thickness of card. When hard, working away from yourself, gently push a sharp-bladed knife along the surface, holding it evenly with both hands and keeping the blade at an angle of 45° to the surface. The chocolate should roll into curls or scrolls.

Orange, lemon or lime decorations

The rind from an orange, lemon or lime is useful in making decorations for sweet dessert dishes.
Twists: Cut the fruit across into thin slices. Using a sharp knife, cut each slice from the edge to the centre. Open the cut and twist each side in opposite directions.
Roses: Using a vegetable peeler or sharp knife, pare away the whole rind of the fruit in one piece. Roll up to form a rose and secure with a cocktail stick.
Wheels: Cut the fruit across into thin slices. Using a sharp knife, notch the edges of the rind at intervals to make attractive wheels.
Boats: Cut the fruit in half lengthways and scoop out the flesh. Notch the edge of the rind with a sharp knife for a decorative design. It may be necessary to cut away a small piece of the skin from the base so that the boat will stand steadily.

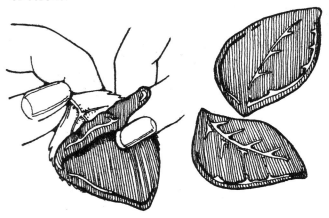

Index